PENGUIN BUSINESS
# GET JOB READY

Vasu Eda is the CEO of RiseSharp, a venture helping college students in India find a job. He founded a human capital management company, Boniva Software, and served as its CEO until its acquisition. He also worked at multinational companies, Alcatel-Lucent and Intel, in corporate strategy, and mergers and acquisitions. Vasu holds an MBA from Columbia University, an MS in computer science from Stevens Institute of Technology, a BE in mechanical engineering from Shivaji University and a diploma in mechanical engineering from Government Polytechnic College, Warangal. He frequently visits colleges as a guest speaker to discuss how to gain valuable experience while in college and, more specifically, how to transition from college to career successfully.

Miriam Schaffer is a writer and college adviser. Her background includes work as a TV news writer, talk show producer and public relations professional. She has published articles in consumer and national trade publications, and written blogs and other content for businesses. As a college adviser and enrolment director for SpanOne College Counselling, Miriam helps students and families navigate the college application process, including choosing colleges that are the best fit for each student and helping with completing college and financial-aid applications. She holds a Bachelor of Arts in English from Skidmore College, New York State.

T0017741

# Get Job Ready

## How to Land Your Dream Job Out of College

### VASU EDA

Foreword by **PALLE RAMA RAO**
Recipient of Padma Shri, Padma Bhushan
and Padma Vibhushan awards

**BUSINESS**

An imprint of Penguin Random House

PENGUIN BUSINESS

USA | Canada | UK | Ireland | Australia
New Zealand | India | South Africa | China

Penguin Business is part of the Penguin Random House group of companies
whose addresses can be found at global.penguinrandomhouse.com

Published by Penguin Random House India Pvt. Ltd
4th Floor, Capital Tower 1, MG Road,
Gurugram 122 002, Haryana, India

First published in Penguin Business by Penguin Random House India 2022

10 9 8 7 6 5 4 3 2 1

ISBN 9780143457411

Typeset in Aldine401 BT by Manipal Technologies Limited, Manipal

www.penguin.co.in

*To all parents facing social and economic challenges,*
*who invest in their children's education as a way*
*to a better future*

# Contents

# Foreword

When I met Vasu Eda for the first time in 2018 to learn about his new venture plans, two things stood out—his genuineness and his passion. He eloquently articulated his interest in addressing the challenges faced by the millions of India's college graduates each year. Today, the majority of college students in India don't have an outcome in hand on the day they collect their certificate. Mr Eda did not see it only as a problem for students, parents and educational institutions, but rather as a problem for the nation.

India is one of the fastest-growing markets in the G20, and its demand for fresh talent is strong. Fuelled by India's global prominence and the market potential, the start-up ecosystem is becoming a significant growth driver in India.

Over the years, so much has been written on career planning and development for professionals. This book, *Get Job Ready*, fills the void that has been left unaddressed for far too long—India's youth and college students.

*Get Job Ready* lays out a clear framework, built on global best practices, to plan, develop and execute one's successful transition from college to career. It comes with concrete plans and steps to address the youth employability issue head-on.

*Get Job Ready* helps readers learn how to gain job-ready experience through academics, on-campus activities, extracurriculars, community service, volunteering, family responsibilities, internships and more. Our youth don't have to go far from their daily lives to gain experience. They can get involved in their educational environment, at home and in the community. Experiences that will result in job-ready skills are easily accessible to them and will help build a foundation for entering the workplace and their career.

28 February 2020                          Palle Rama Rao
Hyderabad

**Palle Rama Rao** is a renowned scientist and the chairman of the Council for the Indian Institute of Science (IISc). He is a recipient of three presidential honours for his distinguished service to the country: the Padma Shri, Padma Bhushan and Padma Vibhushan. In the past, he has held other top positions such as secretary of the Department of Science and Technology, Government of India, and vice chancellor of the University of Hyderabad.

# Introduction

Millions of students graduate from college every year in India. While they proudly accept a certificate, they are quickly disheartened because they are faced with a problem. They do not have a job, or any job prospects. This is a major obstacle not only for the student but also for the parents, the country's colleges, and for the entire society.

Colleges in India have a well-defined academic pathway that leads to graduation, but there is no career pathway that leads to an outcome, job, or career.

*Get Job Ready: How to Land Your Dream Job Out of College* is a non-fiction book targeted to the millions of college students in India. It lays out the steps students need to take while in college so that they are positioned to transition from college to career. It includes topics such as: how to gain job experience through volunteering, internships, class projects, extracurricular activities; creating a cover letter and résumé; handling an interview; creating a LinkedIn profile; and finding a mentor. It also includes pre-built career pathways, step-by-step guides and worksheets based on global best practices. Students who follow the steps laid out in this book will be better positioned to be job ready when they receive a graduation certificate, and will be prepared to take the next step into the working world.

Vasu Eda is uniquely qualified to write this book. He is the co-founder and CEO of RiseSharp, a social impact venture whose mission is to change the college-to-job trajectory for India's college students. RiseSharp helps students plan, prepare and pursue the best path to finding their dream job. Working with higher-education institutions and businesses has provided Vasu with first-hand knowledge of what is required for students to enter the job market. He speaks regularly at colleges on the topic of career planning and explains to faculty, administrators and students the actions students need to take to help them become job ready.

# PART I

# WHY JOB-READINESS MATTERS

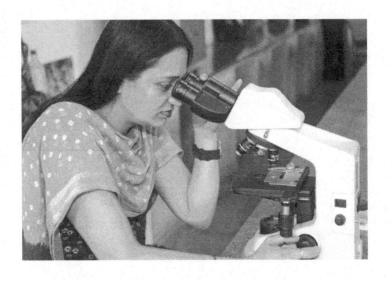

*'A little progress each day adds up to big results.'*

—Anonymous

## Then and Now: How the Workplace Has Changed

The workplace of today is vastly different from the workplace your parents entered. The workplace of yesterday was hierarchical and formal. Employees had specific roles; each worker functioning separately, accomplishing tasks assigned to them. Today's workplace is agile and fluid with a focus on everyone being on a team, working towards a common goal and vision.

'At its core, how we work in the future will be more networked, more devolved, more mobile, more team-based, more project-based, more collaborative, more real-time, and more fluid. Digital technology is having a profound effect on the twenty-first-century organization. It is fundamentally changing the way we work, the way we manage, where we work, how we organize, the products we use, and how we communicate.'—Deloitte survey (sponsored by Facebook).

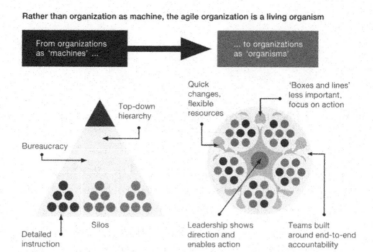

Rather than organization as machine, the agile organization is a living organism

McKinsey&Company

Today's workplace has gone from physical walls to a virtual environment—from the cubicle to collaborative space. In this fluid and agile approach employees work in cohesive, collaborative, cross-functional teams to accomplish the company's common goals. Everyone from the top executive to employees in each and every department shares a common vision and purpose.

Start-ups to Fortune 100 companies have all embraced this agile model. Examples of companies that adhere to this agile model include Amazon, Google, Netflix, Spotify, Tata Consultancy Services and Wipro.

To be successful in today's agile workplace, employees need to work well on a team, have good communication skills, be digitally competent, and be good critical thinkers.

Employers understand and are willing to invest in their employees' continuous development and training when it comes to hard skills such as the intricacies of a new software program, the ins and outs of a database, or specific marketing tactics.

However, employers are reluctant to invest in training employability skills. These skills involve professionalism and a strong work ethic, getting along with others on a team, identifying and solving problems, and being able to communicate well.

Investing your time and effort in developing these skills while in college will make you ready to enter the job market and be successful. Lacking these skills is certain to make the job search and transition from college to career more difficult.

## What is Job-Readiness?

Today's employers want job-ready candidates. There are two factors to being job ready:

1. Having employability skills developed through experiences
2. Being job-search ready with the right tools and preparation

Employability skills are foundational skills that make you employable and successful in any job, in the short and long term. They are skills such as being able to work on a team, communicating well with co-workers, problem-solving, and more. These are usually *not* taught in the classroom or learnt simply by reading books.

As an example, in the workplace of yesterday, if you were applying for a customer service job, and you could follow instructions and speak well on the phone, then you had strong qualifications for the job. In today's workplace, a customer service job involves much more. You need to be digitally competent to handle a chatbot, email, database management and spreadsheets. You need to have clear oral and written communication skills and be a quick thinker to handle complex problems.

Another example from the past—a software engineer could sit all day in his or her cubicle and write code to develop applications, the front-end and the back-end. In today's agile product development environments, an engineer is expected to interact on a daily basis with product management, quality assurance, user interface and others.

In addition, to successfully find and land a job you need to be job-search ready. To become job-search ready, you need a clear understanding of your interests and aspirations, a grasp of industries, a résumé that showcases your skills and can be tailored for various jobs, a well-crafted LinkedIn profile, the ability to write a cover letter that promotes you to employers, good interview skills, and the awareness of how to dress and appear professional.

*Are you participating in a variety of experiences that are helping you to develop employability skills?*

*Are you devoting time to becoming job-search ready?*

Lacking employability skills and job-search readiness will not only make your transition from college to job difficult but can hold you back in your career progression in the future.

In today's business environment, the fact that you are a college graduate is not enough to land a job. With only a certificate in hand, you will find it difficult to open doors in the job market. There are three main qualifications needed for you to successfully transition from college to career:

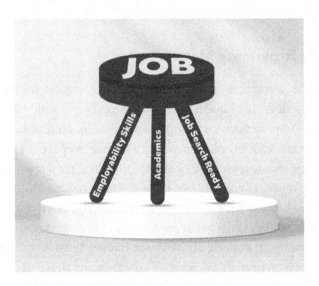

1. Education or academics (e.g., college certificate)
2. Employability skills
3. Job-search readiness

These will make you competitive and successful in today's job market. Those who will be most successful at getting a job will have laid the foundation early on by participating in numerous experiences. It's even possible to begin gaining experiences in secondary school.

If you do not begin prior to college, plan and become involved in experiences early in your college years. This will provide you with the opportunities to develop your employability skills. With a strong list of skills, the next step to become job ready will be to learn to articulate your interests, skills and experiences via your résumé and cover letters, in interviews and in your LinkedIn profile.

## Why Experience Matters

To be attractive to an employer, it's critical to have experiences that have helped you to develop employability skills. Experiences and employability skills are the crucial attributes that employers want, whether you are a recent college graduate or have been out of college for a few years.

However, you do not have to have held a job or an internship to prove to an employer that you have relevant employability skills to succeed in their work environment. You can gain experience without having been employed, through a myriad of ways. You can gain these at your college, your home and in the community.

## Practical Experience Makes You Job Ready

Gaining experience will help you become job ready. While what you learn in the classroom is valuable, you will best retain that knowledge by implementing it in real-life experiences.

# Learning Pyramid
### Average retention rates

5%
Lecture

10% Reading

20% Audiovisual

30% Demonstration

50% Discussion

75% Practice Doing

90% Teach Others

Source: National Training Laboratories, Bethel, Maine

The National Training Laboratories research shows that students retain less than 10 per cent of what they learn in a lecture, but when they practise doing what they've learnt in a real-life situation, the percentage goes up significantly. And, if you take the time to teach someone what you've learnt, the retention is close to 100 per cent.

Retaining the knowledge you've acquired will help you to be job ready and do well in future jobs. During, or after, any type of work experience, it's helpful to expand on this knowledge through reading, online courses, webinars or mentoring other students in some of the skills you've learned.

## 70:20:10 Model for Learning and Development

This is also supported by the 70:20:10 Model for Learning and Development.

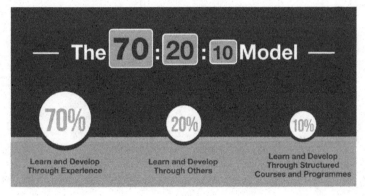

Source: https://charles-jennings.blogspot.com

This model suggests how people learn most effectively and shows that 70 per cent of professional growth comes from learning through doing, or work experiences, 20 per cent comes from interactions with others, and 10 per cent comes from formal education.

## How Are Graduates Evaluated for Hire?

You worked hard in college and were a good student, achieving good grades. While that is important and valuable, you may be surprised to know that, for many employers, grades are not the most important element in choosing whom to hire.

According to Peter Cappelli, a professor at Wharton School of Business, 'Work experience is the crucial attribute that employers want, even for students who have yet to work full-time.'

*The Chronicle of Higher Education reports that when employers make hiring decisions, internships and other employment that occurred during college outweigh a graduate's coursework and grade point average.*

Remember, you do not have to have a job or internship to gain employability skills. The skills that are learnt in a place of business can also be acquired on campus, in the community and at home. Employers will value these experiences because they help you develop critical employability skills.

## Why Do Employers Want Job-Ready Candidates?

Employers want people who are ready to get to work right away. They know that college students are likely to be proficient in hard skills. *Hard skills* are specific abilities such as computer programming, using software programs, web design, accounting, math, database management, mobile and web development, network security, marketing campaign management and project management.

*Employability skills* (sometimes referred to as core skills) are usually not taught in classrooms, but are important to being productive and successful in today's business environment. They include people skills, digital competence and being comfortable with numbers in order to communicate quantifiable information as well as critical thinking, problem-solving, attention to detail, communicating well with others, leadership and teamwork. These skills primarily develop as a result of experiences rather than from a classroom.

## Core Employability Skills

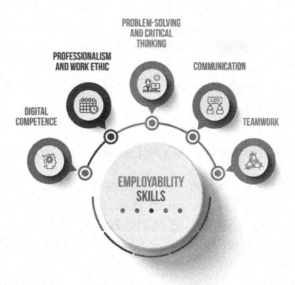

Those without employability skills may find it difficult to gain attention from potential employers.

This concept was further emphasized in an article in the *Wall Street Journal*, 'Employers Find "Soft Skills" Like Critical Thinking in Short Supply.'* The paper conducted a survey of approximately 900 executives in which 92 per cent said that soft skills (employability or core skills), including communication, curiosity and critical thinking, are as important as technical skills. The article reported that 89 per cent of those surveyed said they have a very or somewhat difficult time finding hires with those skills.

*Employers want to be assured that you can successfully transition from student to professional.*

Developing these skills while in college will allow you to include them on your résumé, demonstrate them in interviews and as a result become more attractive to employers.

Here's a closer look at the five core employability skills with actionable ideas:

### Teamwork

Teamwork is a necessary skill to have for almost every industry. Employers look for job candidates who can be team players, because they know they will be getting an employee who will be able to collaborate, communicate, be productive and work to achieve the company's overall

---

\*   Kate Davidson, 'Employers Find "Soft Skills" Like Critical Thinking in Short Supply', *The Wall Street Journal*, 30 August 2016, https://www.wsj.com/articles/employers-find-soft-skills-like-critical-thinking-in-short-supply-1472549400

goals. They want candidates who can demonstrate global/intercultural fluency with experiences that prove their ability to interact and work well with people from all cultures, and who understand cultural differences as well as respect and value the opinions and input from all involved.

Gaining teamwork skills can be achieved through experiences with a leadership role, even of a small group, taking the lead or being part of a team in an organized activity, group or club, perhaps as captain of a sports team, or as an officer in a club or student government.

In addition, in the experiences you're involved in, boost your teamwork skills by developing some of the following:

- Delegating
- Time management
- Listening
- Cooperation
- Commitment
- Creativity
- Research
- Goal setting
- Relationship building
- Empathy

These can be highlighted on your résumé. If you can add quantifiable results from a team experience, such as money raised in a fundraising effort, or increase in visitors to a website you developed, it will maximize your profile.

Keep the above list and quantifiable results in mind and be ready to explain them in a cover letter or an interview.

## Communication

Showcasing your oral and written communication skills begins with your résumé, cover letter and interview. If you have spelling errors and poor grammar, a hiring manager will immediately notice and your résumé or application might quickly be rejected. However, good writing and interview skills will put you on the plus side and make an employer continue to consider you for a position.

Employers want to hire those with good communication skills because they are integral to many aspects of a job. Communication skills are needed daily on a job whether you are writing an email to a client, talking on the phone to clients or team members, writing a report for your project manager, discussing an initiative with your team, sharing your ideas in a meeting or giving a presentation.

You can develop and improve your communication skills through the following experiences:

- Class presentations
- Research projects
- Student government
- Club participation and leadership
- Performing arts
- Public speaking

- Website content writing
- Internship
- Part-time job

Ask classmates and professors to provide feedback and suggestions to improve your communication skills.

When you write your résumé, do not simply state that you have strong communication skills; demonstrate it through experiences and achievements with a statement such as: presented our team's research projects to an audience of professors and members of an academic club.

## Problem-Solving and Critical Thinking

Show employers that you are a creative problem-solver, able to handle situations that do not have a fixed solution. To gain some skills in this area, take some classes that involve hands-on learning or experiential learning. This will provide some experience that will be valuable at a job when things do not go as planned or obstacles are faced. Also, try things that are out of your comfort zone, such as participating in a club or organization that is not in your area of academic focus. For example, an engineering student might join a debate club to gain skills in public speaking and persuasion.

Having strong numeracy skills does not mean that you have to be a math whiz or become an accountant or scientist. To be effective at many jobs, you will need to be able to analyse numerical information to draw conclusions and make decisions. In addition to having a basic understanding of math, strong numeracy skills imply that you are capable of organizing information, understanding charts and graphs, budgeting, scheduling, drawing conclusions from data and making calculations.

If you were involved in a research project or worked as a lab assistant, highlight on your résumé how you analysed data to draw conclusions, or used graphs and charts in a report. Or, if you were responsible for a club's budget, include budget management as a skill on your résumé.

## Digital Competence

Almost all jobs require a level of digital expertise, and the need to be digitally competent will certainly continue to increase as the world becomes more digital. Being digitally competent means that you have the knowledge, skill and ability when using technology to be competent at the tasks you are responsible for in your job. Through the use of technology, you are able to solve problems, communicate, collaborate and manage information required to be successful.

In most jobs today, regardless of the industry, employees need to be competent with Microsoft Office including Outlook, Word, Excel, PowerPoint, Teams, Yammer or other similar software. If you do not know your way around these tools, it will be critical to get up to speed for most jobs.

Beyond the basics, it will also be helpful to have some knowledge of coding, video editing and creating infographics.

Digital competence also means you are effectively managing your online image on LinkedIn as well as making sure you have nothing inappropriate on other social media sites. Hiring managers are very likely to research you online. You want to appear professional and make a good impression.

Your digital skills can be listed on your résumé. If you have used your skills to build a website, create a successful email marketing campaign, increase awareness of a company through its social media or used your digital skills to help run a family business, be sure to include this information on your résumé.

## *Professionalism and Work Ethic*

No matter how strong your teamwork, communication, problem-solving, critical thinking and digital competence skills are, if you are not professional and unable to demonstrate a strong work ethic, you will not be valued in the workplace.

Professionalism is demonstrated by being someone who people want to work with by arriving at work on time, displaying a good attitude, taking advice and direction well, not gossiping about co-workers and dressing appropriately for the job. As a professional, you are able to effectively manage your time, meet deadlines and be accountable for your actions.

Having a good work ethic means that you are reliable and responsible, work well with others towards a common goal and are committed to the projects you are assigned—even going beyond what is expected of you.

Professionalism and work ethic can be demonstrated to employers by letting them know that you have been able to successfully manage and prioritize your classes, studies, leadership positions and other outside activities.

If you are an athlete, a coach can perhaps provide a reference stating that you were always on time, and were a good team member and someone who was looked up to by others.

For those who held an internship or tutoring position, you can let a potential employer know that you were always on time, completed all work assigned to you and that you were well regarded by others in the company or organization.

*Employers want to know that you can easily transition from life as a student to the professional world, so always be on the lookout for things you can do to improve your employability skills.*

'*The only source of knowledge is experience.*'

—Albert Einstein

## WORKSHEET: My Dream Jobs

What is your dream job? Is it to work at a company such as Google, Amazon, Infosys, IBM, Wipro, a start-up or somewhere else? What industry do you want to work in? Is your goal to work in IT, healthcare, hospitality, education, journalism, banking, marketing, or do you envision yourself working in another field?

Dream big. List roles and/or the companies or organizations where you would like to work:

1._____

2._____

3._____

4._____

5._____

**Notes:**

_____

_____

_____

_____

# PART II

# HOW TO DEVELOP
# EMPLOYABILITY SKILLS

'*Opportunities are not offered. They must be wrested and worked for. And this calls for perseverance . . . and courage.*'
—Indira Gandhi

## How Will You Develop Employability Skills?

Employability skills can be developed through a myriad of experiences. Gaining these experiences while in college will help you strengthen your profile and make you more attractive to employers. Experiences come in all shapes and sizes. Your college and the community offer many opportunities to gain experience and develop critical employability skills.

| Academic Experiences | Case studies, class projects, field trips, dissertations, speaking engagements, research projects, academic competitions, group volunteer initiatives |
|---|---|
| On-Campus Experiences | Research assistant, teaching assistant, peer tutor, residential hall adviser, campus ambassador, lab assistant, library assistant |
| Extracurricular Experiences | Student government, visual and performing arts, community service, academic clubs, professional clubs, sports clubs, hobbies and special interests, media, religious groups, recreation and fitness, service and volunteerism |
| External Experiences | Job shadowing, summer internship, part-time or full-time job, volunteering, family responsibilities |

*There is no right or wrong experience. It's more important to pick experiences based on your interests and commit to them. Commitment helps build employability skills.*

Here are some ways to get started on gaining a variety of experiences to help get job ready and increase your appeal to employers:

## Class Projects and Research Projects

Academic projects offer great opportunities to develop many critical employability skills. Whether it is working with your classmates on a team project, conducting research for a class, presenting your findings to a class or participating in an academic field trip—all of these are examples of ways to help build your skills.

Self-directed research projects help go deeper into your area of interest and strengthen your résumé. Research can be done in any area of study, from engineering to humanities to social sciences.

Listing these types of activities and projects on your résumé will help employers become aware of your skills.

When participating in class work or projects related to your job goals, keep a record with a few bullet points about what you learnt, what you did, any results and, if possible, a web link that can show more information. If you won any awards for the project, be sure to refer to them.

For those who will be seeking a position in a field such as biochemistry or other sciences in which professors are doing research, a good way to gain experience is by assisting professors with their research. Talk with professors or contact the offices of department heads to learn if any professors are seeking a student assistant. This experience can also result in high-quality letters of recommendation and referrals to potential employers.

## WORKSHEET: My Class Projects and Research Projects

List class or research projects that you have completed and indicate one or more of the core employability skills.

**Project:**_____

### Core Employability Skills You Have Developed (select one or more):

☐ Teamwork  ☐ Communication  ☐ Problem-solving
☐ Digital Competence  ☐ Work Ethic

**Project:**_____

### Core Employability Skills You Have Developed (select one or more):

☐ Teamwork  ☐ Communication  ☐ Problem-solving
☐ Digital Competence  ☐ Work Ethic

**Project:**_____

### Core Employability Skills You Have Developed (select one or more):

☐ Teamwork  ☐ Communication  ☐ Problem-solving
☐ Digital Competence  ☐ Work Ethic

**Notes:**

_____

_____

_____

_____

_____

_____

_____

_____

_____

_____

_____

_____

_____

## *Extracurricular Activities*

While in college, extracurricular activities are amazing avenues to build core employability skills. Extracurricular activities are activities that fall outside your regular academic work.

In addition to helping you build necessary skills, extracurricular activities offer additional benefits. They can expand your thinking and perspective, increase your self-confidence, and build a network of friends. There is no one best extracurricular activity. What is best for you may be different from what is best for your classmate. Find an activity that you can enjoy and that helps you grow. A number of research studies have shown that students who participate in extracurricular activities perform better academically.

Here are a few examples of extracurricular activities to help showcase and develop your employability skills:

- Leadership in student government
- Visual and performing arts participation
- Community service volunteering or leadership
- Caretaking for family members
- Academic clubs
- Clubs representing professions and associations
- Participation, awards or outstanding achievements in hobbies and special interests
- Tutoring experience
- Sports team member, captain or coach
- Research projects
- Leadership or other participation in on-campus media

Don't hesitate to use your extracurricular activities to highlight your accomplishments and to illustrate your successes. Have you started an on-campus club or had a significant role in one? Do your extracurriculars involve skills such as leadership as head of a club, managing events, marketing, writing, website design and development, creating policies, such as in student government or research projects? Are you on a cricket, volleyball, badminton or soccer team? Are you the captain of a team? Do you coach younger students? Do you have significant responsibility for taking care of a family member? All these skills can be important in a professional environment and can impress an employer.

If there's an area that you want to be involved in, or a leadership role that you want to take on, and the opportunity doesn't exist on campus, then create it. This will show future employers that you can take initiative, are a creative thinker, a leader, and are not afraid to take on a challenge.

## WORKSHEET: My Extracurricular Activities

List extracurricular activities that you have been involved in and indicate one or more of the core employability skills.

**Extracurricular Activity:**

_____

**Core Employability Skills You Have Developed (select one or more):**

☐ Teamwork  ☐ Communication  ☐ Problem-solving
☐ Digital Competence  ☐ Work Ethic

**Extracurricular Activity:**

_____

**Core Employability Skills You Have Developed (select one or more):**

☐ Teamwork  ☐ Communication  ☐ Problem-solving
☐ Digital Competence  ☐ Work Ethic

**Extracurricular Activity:**

_____

**Core Employability Skills You Have Developed (select one or more):**

☐ Teamwork  ☐ Communication  ☐ Problem-solving
☐ Digital Competence  ☐ Work Ethic

**Notes:**

_____

_____

_____

_____

_____

_____

_____

_____

_____

_____

_____

_____

_____

_____

*Family Responsibilities*

Employability skills may be part of your everyday life. Does your family own a business where you've worked with a set schedule? Does your job role at the business include responsibilities such as maintaining the website, providing database management, creating invoices, scheduling deliveries, or do you have regular contact with customers? These types of roles can be included on your résumé to show skills such as communication, digital competence and a good work ethic.

Perhaps your family responsibilities include taking care of an elderly relative or other family member on a regular basis. Are you cooking meals, taking care of siblings, making sure an elderly person stays safe in the home, accompanying a relative to regular medical appointments, or making sure an elderly person takes their medication regularly? These responsibilities should not be ignored. They show a strong level of character and can be included on your résumé to highlight your problem-solving, communication and work ethic skills.

## WORKSHEET: My Family Responsibilities

List your family responsibilities that relate to one or more of the core employability skills.

**Family Responsibility:**

_____

**Core Employability Skills You Have Developed (select one or more):**

☐ Teamwork  ☐ Communication  ☐ Problem-solving
☐ Digital Competence  ☐ Work Ethic

**Family Responsibility:**

_____

**Core Employability Skills You Have Developed (select one or more):**

☐ Teamwork  ☐ Communication  ☐ Problem-solving
☐ Digital Competence  ☐ Work Ethic

**Family Responsibility:**

_____

**Core Employability Skills You Have Developed (select one or more):**

☐ Teamwork  ☐ Communication  ☐ Problem-solving
☐ Digital Competence  ☐ Work Ethic

**Notes:**

_____

_____

_____

_____

_____

_____

_____

_____

_____

_____

_____

_____

_____

## Freelancing

Freelance jobs are an excellent way to gain experience. Most freelancing jobs allow you to work on your own schedule. You usually do not have to go to an office or other workplace.

The freelance projects you complete should be included on your résumé. The people that you work for can also be considered to provide references for jobs you apply to.

Two websites where you can find freelancing jobs are Upwork (https://www.upwork.com) and Fiverr (https://www.fiverr.com/).

These sites have numerous jobs posted daily from people and companies worldwide that are seeking help in a multitude of categories, including data entry, admin support, virtual assistant, graphic design, content writing, public relations, data science, programming and tech, video and animation, social media marketing, web design, search engine optimization and many more.

You will need to make a profile. Add as much detail as possible focusing on your main skills. Until you begin earning and have a good reputation, set a low hourly rate to be competitive. When you see a job that interests you, apply for it. Write a separate cover letter or an email message for each job you apply to, specifically addressing the project you are bidding on.

In addition, an employer can invite you to apply for a project. You are allowed to say 'no' to an invitation.

If you receive a message from someone whose job you've applied to, or been invited to, reply to them as soon as possible. Ask any further questions to clarify the project requirements and expectations, and provide them with any additional information that might not be included on your profile or in your cover letter.

While some jobs do not pay very much, it is worth doing them to add to your résumé.

There are many talented freelancers on Upwork and Fiverr, which can initially make it difficult to get hired. Once you have successfully finished some projects and received good reviews, it will become easier.

It's best to apply to jobs that are from people (clients) who have high ratings to avoid any scams.

## WORKSHEET: My Freelance Work

List your freelance work that reflects one or more of the core employability skills.

**Freelance Work:**_____

**Core Employability Skills You Have Developed (select one or more):**

☐ Teamwork  ☐ Communication  ☐ Problem-solving
☐ Digital Competence  ☐ Work Ethic

**Freelance Work:**_____

**Core Employability Skills You Have Developed (select one or more):**

☐ Teamwork  ☐ Communication  ☐ Problem-solving
☐ Digital Competence  ☐ Work Ethic

**Freelance Work:**_____

**Core Employability Skills You Have Developed (select one or more):**

☐ Teamwork  ☐ Communication  ☐ Problem-solving
☐ Digital Competence  ☐ Work Ethic

**Notes:**

_____

_____

_____

_____

_____

_____

_____

_____

_____

_____

_____

_____

_____

## Academic Tutoring

Commitment, communication, handling challenges, time management and work ethic are some of the employability skills that you can gain by being an academic tutor. You can offer your tutoring services to students in your community or at your college, to friends and family, or through an online tutoring service.

To be successful as a tutor, you will need to present information clearly, listen attentively, keep students engaged and be a confident leader. All of these attributes are employability skills that can be communicated to a hiring manager or other decision maker when applying for jobs.

Take the following steps to become a tutor:

1. Decide what age of students you want to tutor: Will you work best with young children, secondary school students, college students or adults?
2. Choose the subjects you want to tutor: What subjects are you best in, which you can teach your clients?
3. Get to know your student: What areas of a subject does your student need help with? How does your student learn best? Games? PowerPoint? Textbooks? Use their learning strengths to impart your knowledge.
4. Choose a location: If you are not tutoring through a tutoring centre, will you tutor at the student's home, a public location or online?

Keep track of your students' quantifiable results.

Promote your academic tutoring experience by explaining your results to employers. If you started your own tutoring business, you can let employers know how you took the initiative to get clients, whether through a website, online advertising, social media, referrals or other means.

## WORKSHEET: Academic Tutoring

List tutoring positions you've held that reflect one or more of the core employability skills.

**Academic Tutoring Work:**

_____

**Core Employability Skills You Have Developed (select one or more):**

☐ Teamwork  ☐ Communication  ☐ Problem-solving
☐ Digital Competence  ☐ Work Ethic

**Academic Tutoring Work:**

_____

**Core Employability Skills You Have Developed (select one or more):**

☐ Teamwork  ☐ Communication  ☐ Problem-solving
☐ Digital Competence  ☐ Work Ethic

**Academic Tutoring Work:**

_____

**Core Employability Skills You Have Developed (select one or more):**

☐ Teamwork  ☐ Communication  ☐ Problem-solving
☐ Digital Competence  ☐ Work Ethic

**Notes:**

_____

_____

_____

_____

_____

_____

_____

_____

_____

_____

_____

_____

## On-Campus Jobs and Experiences

Another way to gain experience and develop critical employability skills is through on-campus job opportunities. Examples include:

- Teaching assistant
- Peer tutor
- Residential hall adviser
- Admissions office ambassador
- Lab assistant
- Library assistant
- Administrative assistant
- IT assistant
- Career services peer adviser
- Online news editor/writer/reporter

All of these are experiences that can take place on your college campus, and will make you more attractive to employers by providing you with the following employability skills:

- Dedication and commitment
- Teamwork and collaboration
- Time management
- Digital competence
- Handling challenges
- Professionalism
- Communication skills
- Confidence

## WORKSHEET: On-Campus Jobs

List the on-campus jobs you've held that reflect one or more of the core employability skills.

**On-Campus Job:**_____

**Core Employability Skills You Have Developed (select one or more):**

☐ Teamwork  ☐ Communication  ☐ Problem-solving
☐ Digital Competence  ☐ Work Ethic

**On-Campus Job:**_____

**Core Employability Skills You Have Developed (select one or more):**

☐ Teamwork  ☐ Communication  ☐ Problem-solving
☐ Digital Competence  ☐ Work Ethic

**On-Campus Job:**_____

**Core Employability Skills You Have Developed (select one or more):**

☐ Teamwork  ☐ Communication  ☐ Problem-solving
☐ Digital Competence  ☐ Work Ethic

**Notes:**

_____

_____

_____

_____

_____

_____

_____

_____

_____

_____

_____

_____

_____

## *Community Service*

Going beyond your campus to be involved in community service is an accessible and excellent way to gain experiences, and make a positive impact in society. It provides you with a path to develop employability skills such as dedication, commitment, teamwork, dealing with challenges, communication skills and confidence.

When choosing a community service activity, find one that has some connection to your interests and the skills you want to develop. You might choose to be involved in a community service project to help children, the elderly, the disabled or the environment. Opportunities might be listed in your college's training and placement office, or found through your local non-profit organizations and non-governmental organizations, and through online search.

Depending on the type of community service activity you become involved in, it will be helpful to keep track of your quantifiable accomplishments. Include them on your résumé and refer to them in job interviews. Examples of this might be: a successful fundraising campaign; the number of students you tutored and any increase in their competencies; a budget you managed or reviewed; office work completed; organizational tasks such as organizing an event for a library, healthcare clinic, or other business or organization.

Here are fifteen ideas for community service activities:

1. Coach a sports team at a school.
2. Collect clothing for those in need.
3. Collect toys for children in a hospital.
4. Read to a visually-impaired person.
5. Visit patients at a nursing home.
6. Help deliver meals to the sick or elderly.
7. Organize an after-school programme for children at a library.
8. Organize a book drive to donate books to a library.
9. Provide musical entertainment to children in a hospital or patients in a nursing home.
10. Help with home repairs for the elderly or disabled.
11. Organize a crew to clean up a park or other public area.
12. Volunteer to tutor at a school or after-school programme.
13. Organize a fundraiser to support a charity.
14. Help the elderly or disabled get to medical appointments.
15. Take care of animals at an animal shelter.

## WORKSHEET: Community Service Work

List community service work you've done that reflects one or more of the core employability skills.

**Community Service:**

_____

**Core Employability Skills You Have Developed (select one or more):**

☐ Teamwork  ☐ Communication  ☐ Problem-solving
☐ Digital Competence  ☐ Work Ethic

**Community Service:**

_____

**Core Employability Skills You Have Developed (select one or more):**

☐ Teamwork  ☐ Communication  ☐ Problem-solving
☐ Digital Competence  ☐ Work Ethic

**Community Service:**

_____

**Core Employability Skills You Have Developed (select one or more):**

☐ Teamwork  ☐ Communication  ☐ Problem-solving
☐ Digital Competence  ☐ Work Ethic

**Notes:**

_____

_____

_____

_____

_____

_____

_____

_____

_____

_____

_____

_____

_____

## *Job Shadowing*

A job shadow provides the opportunity to follow a professional on the job. This will give you a better understanding of what the job entails on a daily basis. A job shadow can be for one day or longer. Participating in a job shadow will show employers that you are serious about gaining knowledge regarding your future career. A job shadow experience can turn into an internship or full-time opportunity in the future.

You can learn only so much by reading books or watching videos. The best way to experience what it means to be a software engineer, customer service executive, digital marketing representative, business development manager or any other role is by job shadowing someone in the role. In addition, job shadowing will help you prepare for interviews.

## How to Find Job Shadow Opportunities

To obtain a job shadow, it's helpful if you know someone at the company you're targeting. Contact that person and explain that you're interested in their career and would like to job shadow them or another individual at the company for whatever length of time is most convenient.

If you don't know anyone at the company, contact the human resources department, explain your interest in the industry and ask if they provide job shadow opportunities.

## Finding Job Shadow Opportunities

1. Check with your college's training and placement office to see if they have a list of opportunities.
2. Call or email someone you know at a company or contact the human resources department to tell them you'd like to job shadow.
3. Check job websites. Those that regularly hire interns may let you job shadow.

## Planning for Your Job Shadow

Once you've landed a job shadow, prepare yourself by doing the following before the job shadow begins:

1. Review the company's website to gain basic facts about the company, its employees, and its mission and values.
2. If you know in advance who you will be job shadowing, research their role so you have some understanding of what they do.

3.   Have some questions ready to ask the person you'll be
     job shadowing. Examples:

- Why did you choose this job?
- What do you like about your job?
- What are the challenges you face?
- What employability skills are needed to get an
  entry-level position in your company?
- What should I be focusing on in college to get a
  job in this industry?

## The Job Shadow Day

On the day of your job shadow, be prepared and focus on
being involved:

- Know the street address of the company or
  organization.
- Allow for extra time to get there to avoid being late.
- Dress appropriately for the job, or if in doubt, dress as
  though you are going to a job interview.
- Bring a notepad or tablet for note-taking.
- Do not be preoccupied with texting your friends or
  looking at social media on your phone.
- Agree to participate in every activity presented to you.
- Try to meet as many people as possible and ask for
  business cards. The people you meet may be good
  future contacts for you.
- Remember you are in a workplace and while you
  would want to meet many people, be aware that they

are working and may not be able to spend a lot of time
with you.

- If you are invited to a restaurant, do not order the
  most expensive item, but order food and a drink that
  are similar in price to what your host or others order.

## After Your Job Shadow

Acknowledge the experience by doing the following:

- Send a thank-you note to the person who hosted you
  and others who spent a considerable amount of time
  with you as well as those you want to stay in contact
  with.
- In the thank-you note, refer to one or two specific
  activities that you enjoyed participating in.
- Keep the business cards you collected in a database or
  file, in order to contact people in the future for more
  information, or to ask questions, including inquiring
  about job opportunities.

## CHECKLIST: Job Shadowing

### Pre-job Shadow

☐ Research companies where you would like to job shadow.

☐ Check with your college's training and placement office for job shadow opportunities.

☐ Email or call companies where you would like to job shadow:

    ☐ Contact people you know or have been referred to.

    ☐ Email the human resources department.

### Before the Job Shadow Day

☐ Review the company's website.

☐ Research employees and their roles.

☐ Prepare questions to ask.

☐ Find out the company's address and how long it will take to get there.

☐ Plan what you will wear.

☐ Have a notepad or tablet ready to take notes.

### The Job Shadow Day

☐ Schedule enough time to get to the job shadow to avoid being late.

☐ Be friendly and attentive. Put your phone away.

☐ Take notes.

☐ Ask questions.

- ☐ Get business cards.
- ☐ If you are invited to a restaurant, pay attention to what others order and order a similarly priced item.

## After the Job Shadow

- ☐ Write and send thank-you notes.
- ☐ Put contact names in a database or file.

## WORKSHEET: Job Shadow

List any job shadows you've held that reflect one or more of the core employability skills.

**Job Shadow:**_____

**Core Employability Skills You Have Developed (select one or more):**

☐ Teamwork  ☐ Communication  ☐ Problem-solving
☐ Digital Competence  ☐ Work Ethic

**Job Shadow:** _____

**Core Employability Skills You Have Developed (select one or more):**

☐ Teamwork  ☐ Communication  ☐ Problem-solving
☐ Digital Competence  ☐ Work Ethic

**Job Shadow:**_____

**Core Employability Skills You Have Developed (select one or more):**

☐ Teamwork  ☐ Communication  ☐ Problem-solving
☐ Digital Competence  ☐ Work Ethic

**Notes:**

_____

_____

_____

_____

_____

_____

_____

_____

_____

_____

_____

_____

_____

*Internships*

An internship is a temporary position (usually a few weeks to a few months) in which a student or other pre-professional works at a company or organization. Some internships are paid and some are not.

## Five Benefits of Internships

1. Provides first-hand experience in the working world
2. Builds your résumé
3. Helps you decide if a particular career or job is something you enjoy and a good fit for you
4. Builds your professional network
5. Introduces you to people who can be a reference

## Getting an Internship

You are a good candidate if you can demonstrate that you have relevant skills and can relate your experiences to the internship requirements.

When you are ready to apply for internships, follow these six steps and you'll be on the path to landing a position that aligns with your career goals and helps you to become job ready:

1. *Start Looking Early*
   Don't wait to begin looking. It's important to start at least six months in advance of when you plan to begin your internship.

2. *Network with Students*
   Talk to fellow students who have previously held internships to find opportunities and to learn about their experiences. Ask them if they can refer you to the decision maker and perhaps even put in a good word for you.

3. *Join a Club*
   You can join a club or professional association relevant to the industry in which you are seeking an internship. Check whether there is a membership fee for students. You will meet business people who may be able to direct you to internship opportunities. Stay in contact with the people you meet through email and begin to build a professional network. In addition,

some clubs and associations may post internships on their websites.

4.  *Write Professionally*
    Don't lose out on an opportunity because of poor communication skills. Make sure when communicating via email with a potential employer that your writing is professional. Ask someone with job experience, such as a family member, friend or teacher to review your email before sending it. There are many websites with writing tips, such as risesharp. com, careeraddict.com and thebalancecareers.com.

5.  *Create a Résumé*
    Most employers will expect to receive your résumé when you apply for an internship position. Even if you have not held any type of job, there are still things you can highlight on your résumé to demonstrate your skills. If certain skills will be valuable for the type of internship you are seeking, and they are not part of your coursework, then consider earning a certificate on a site such as Lynda.com or Coursera. To show that you have had some success, try to land a freelance gig on a site such as Upwork.com, Freelancer.com or Fiverr.com. If you have any volunteer experience, include it, highlighting any hard skills or employability skills that you have acquired. Make sure to have your résumé reviewed by a friend with job experience or at your college's training and placement office. More details on creating a résumé is covered in Part III.

6. *Create a LinkedIn Account*

   Create an account on LinkedIn that highlights your skills and experiences. You can use LinkedIn to network and find jobs, internships or other opportunities, although networking face-to-face with people outside of social media may prove more effective.

## Zeroing in on the Internship of Your Dreams

Think about the companies you would like to intern with and make a list of them. Read about them on their websites; follow them on LinkedIn, Facebook and Twitter.

Look at the 'Careers' or 'Job Openings' pages on their sites to see if any internships are offered and the requirements they are seeking. If you don't know the names of companies that offer the type of jobs you're interested in, visit the college's training and placement office, or ask professors for advice.

You can also do research on LinkedIn. Click on the 'Jobs' tab and in the search bar, type in something such as 'biotech internship' and then the name of a city.

*CHECKLIST: Internship*

Internships help you grow by providing opportunities to learn and network while putting your education and knowledge to work.

Internship Position: _____

Internship Organization: _____

Internship Location: _____

Manager's Name: _____

Manager's Email: _____

Manager's Phone: _____

Start Date: _____

End Date: _____

## Before Starting Your Internship

☐ Know your start date, time and location.

☐ Find out who you will be meeting upon arrival at the location.

☐ Plan your transportation (Tip: Make sure you arrive on time, preferably early).

## During Your Internship

☐ Learn, Learn, Learn. Internships are tremendous learning opportunities.

☐ Add your internship to your LinkedIn profile. Include details about your role and responsibilities.

☐ Project a professional image by dressing appropriately, arriving on time and being responsible.

☐ Add your manager and colleagues to your LinkedIn profile (Tip: Add only people with whom you have interacted).

☐ Take advantage of opportunities to learn from others and seek guidance.

☐ Research employees and their roles.

## After Your Internship

☐ Send thank-you letters to your manager and others who helped you. Feel free to ask if they would be open to providing a recommendation letter or being a reference in future.

☐ Update your résumé and LinkedIn profile. Add your internship, with details about your responsibilities, projects you worked on and accomplishments.

☐ Discuss your internship experience and learnings with your training and placement office, mentor and family.

## WORKSHEET: Internships

List any internships you've held that reflect one or more of the core employability skills.

**Internship:**_____

**Core Employability Skills You Have Developed (select one or more):**

☐ Teamwork ☐ Communication ☐ Problem-solving
☐ Digital Competence ☐ Work Ethic

**Internship:**_____

**Core Employability Skills You Have Developed (select one or more):**

☐ Teamwork ☐ Communication ☐ Problem-solving
☐ Digital Competence ☐ Work Ethic

**Internship:**_____

**Core Employability Skills You Have Developed (select one or more):**

☐ Teamwork ☐ Communication ☐ Problem-solving
☐ Digital Competence ☐ Work Ethic

**Notes:**

_____

_____

_____

_____

_____

_____

_____

_____

_____

_____

_____

_____

_____

*Volunteering*

Look for volunteering opportunities that are relevant to your major or career goals, which will provide valuable job-ready experiences to build needed employability skills. Volunteering will give you an opportunity to get some experience and earn you a source for job references that can communicate positive comments about your abilities. In your volunteer position, exhibit qualities such as being a good worker, motivated and a quick learner. These are attributes that will impress an employer.

Volunteering can also help you build your network, providing you with more contacts that may be able to help you in your job search.

## Volunteer Your Way to a Job

*Volunteering can, and often does, turn into full-time employment, since many organizations first look internally when paid positions open up. Performing a volunteer job to the best of your ability will put you on their radar, and knowing how the organization operates will give you a boost in the interview process.*

—Source: http://www.good-deeds-day.org

## What to Consider When Seeking a Volunteer Position

1. Think about the type of work you want to do in the future and seek a volunteer position that will provide you with some of the employability skills you'll need.
2. Do online research or ask at your college's training and placement office to learn about available volunteer opportunities.
3. Choose an organization whose values match yours and that you will feel committed to being part of.
4. Consider how much time you have available. Is it one day a week? Twice a week, or more? For how many months will you volunteer? Some organizations might request that you commit for a specific length of time, so before agreeing to volunteer, make sure you understand the time commitment.

## How Volunteering Can Help You in the Future

There are long-term benefits to volunteering that can help you land a job in the future. Volunteering can help you:

- Learn new skills and increase your list of employability skills, including project management, problem-solving, time management, sales, writing and communication skills, interpersonal skills, being an effective team member and more.
- Make business contacts with those who are either also volunteering or employed by the organization.
- Boost your résumé by listing your volunteer experience and explaining how the role contributed to employability skills.

## WORKSHEET: Volunteering

List any volunteer positions you've held that reflect one or more of the core employability skills.

**Volunteer Position:**_____

**Core Employability Skills You Have Developed (select one or more):**

☐ Teamwork ☐ Communication ☐ Problem-solving
☐ Digital Competence ☐ Work Ethic

**Volunteer Position:**_____

**Core Employability Skills You Have Developed (select one or more):**

☐ Teamwork ☐ Communication ☐ Problem-solving
☐ Digital Competence ☐ Work Ethic

**Volunteer Position:**_____

**Core Employability Skills You Have Developed (select one or more):**

☐ Teamwork ☐ Communication ☐ Problem-solving
☐ Digital Competence ☐ Work Ethic

**Notes:**

_____

_____

_____

_____

_____

_____

_____

_____

_____

_____

_____

_____

## Online Resources

In addition to your college's placement office, family and friends, there are many online resources to find opportunities. If you don't know the names of companies that you want to target, or aren't finding them through your network, look at online professional sites such as LinkedIn and job boards.

## Choose Quality over Quantity

Rather than having a long list of activities and projects that you participate in, it is more impactful to have one or two that you are committed to. Being able to show that you've developed a depth of experience and had meaningful experiences in a few areas will help you to stand out from the competition. A great way to demonstrate to employers your job readiness and employability skills is through dedication and achievement of select experiences.

*Not sure where to start to gain experience to develop employability skills and get job ready?*

## Six Tips to Help You Get Started

1. Meet with your training and placement office to develop a plan of action.
2. Ask professors for their advice on who to talk to and how to uncover internships and other professional opportunities.

3. Ask friends and family to introduce you to their contacts.
4. Join campus organizations or sports teams.
5. Contact organizations to determine if they have community service and volunteering opportunities.
6. Sign up on websites such as Upwork.com or Fiverr.com for freelance opportunities.

*'Our goals can only be reached through the vehicle of a plan, in which we must fervently believe, and upon which we must vigorously act. There is no other route to success.'*

—Pablo Picasso

# PART III

# HOW TO GET JOB-SEARCH READY

*'Ability is what you're capable of doing. Motivation determines what you do. Attitude determines how well you do it.'*

—Lou Holtz

With your strong academic record and list of employability skills, you are now ready to create the tools to help you to successfully find and land a job. To become job-search ready, you need a clear understanding of your interests and aspirations, a grasp of industries, a résumé that showcases your skills and that can be tailored for various jobs, a well-crafted LinkedIn profile, the ability to write a cover letter that promotes you to employers, good interview skills, and the awareness of how to dress and appear professional.

## The Critical Elements to Becoming Job-Search Ready

### The Résumé

If you have participated in any of the experiences described in the previous sections, such as job shadowing, volunteering, class projects, research, on-campus jobs, internships, working in your family's business, taking on family responsibilities or other experiences, then you will have content for your résumé.

It's standard practice for employers to require that you submit a résumé when applying for a job.

## The Main Parts of a Résumé

Having a well-written résumé that is specifically targeted to the position you are applying to can increase the possibility of a successful outcome. Instead of sending a generic résumé, revise it for each position you apply to so that your skills are a close match to what's described in the job posting. The goal is for your résumé to stand out from the competition, providing you a better chance of landing in the 'yes' pile and earning an invite to interview. Understanding the main parts of a résumé will help you to create your own and achieve positive results.

## Your résumé should include the following:

*Contact Information*

Name • home address • email address • phone number • LinkedIn profile

*Objective or Summary*

Brief summary of your professional accomplishments and career goals

*Education*

Degree • college • graduation date • GPA • projects

*Experience*

Job title • company • employment dates • explanation of your role • contributions and achievements

*Skills, Awards and Interests*

List employability skills and hard skills
Award name • organization giving award • year received • description of award
List key interests

*Additional Information*

If you have a website or portfolio that is relevant to the job you are applying to, such as one that involves graphic design, video work, research findings, writing, programming skills or web design, include a link to the site in your additional information section.

## Descriptions of Parts of the Résumé

*Contact Information*

It's common sense, but job applicants sometimes forget to include their contact information or put it at the bottom of the page. You want to make it easy for employers to find the information to contact you. At the top of your résumé, include:

- Your name
- Home city
- Email address
- Phone number
- Link to your LinkedIn profile

*Objective or Summary*

It is not necessary to include an objective in your résumé. If you do include one, the objective should have a sentence about the type of position you are seeking, highlight your employability skills, and grab the employer's attention by stating something such as a high grade point average or relevant experiences.

Place the objective below your contact info. It needs to relate to the position for which you are applying. In many cases, companies use an automated system to scan résumés before they go to the hiring manager. Include keywords and key phrases that are included in the job description to get past the automation and into the hands of decision makers.

*Objective or Summary Examples*

*To obtain a civil engineering internship that will utilize my math and design skills. A 4.0 GPA is evidence of my hard work and commitment to succeeding as an engineer.*

*Seeking a position in the IT industry that will allow me to expand my knowledge. As a top-performing student, I have tutored students and completed projects that correspond to this internship.*

*To obtain a position with <name of company> where I can use my skills in economics and marketing.*

*A graduate of computer engineering at <name of college>, with proven mobile application development experience, seeking a software engineering opportunity with a start-up.*

*To obtain a customer service position that will utilize my strength as a strong team member, good oral and written communication skills, and professionalism.*

*An MBA graduate with specialization in human resources is seeking an entry level position in the field of human capital management.*

*An entrepreneurial nursing degree candidate, with clinical internship at a multi-specialty hospital, is looking for a full-time opportunity in the healthcare industry.*

*To use my strong communication and critical thinking skills to gain a position in digital marketing and product management to drive product success and process efficiency.*

*Experience*

Your résumé needs to include an experience section. This typically includes describing the experiences you've had whether they are volunteer or community service work, working for a company or family business, club activities, leadership positions, research projects or research assistant, or other experiences. If you don't have academic, on-campus, extracurricular or external experiences, then use this section to expand and focus on your employability skills and any accomplishments that have resulted from your education that are relevant to the job you are applying for.

*Education*

In the education section, list the educational institutions you attended, your graduation date and the degree you received. If you took relevant professional development courses include those and any certifications you have earned. If you have completed any projects include those too, including the contributions and results.

*Skills, Awards and Interests*

Employers place an emphasis on employability skills. Use examples from any of your experiences: class projects, research activities, community service, volunteering, on-campus jobs, job shadows, internships, tutoring, club leadership, student government and family responsibilities. This may help improve your chances of being considered for the job. In addition, include your hard skills. Examples: computer programming, web design, accounting, writing, legal knowledge, languages you are fluent in and administrative skills.

Include any honours or awards you have received and a brief description of the work accomplished that earned you the award as well as a description of the award. These could be awards or honours for academic, work-related or extracurricular achievements.

## Formatting

Format your résumé so that it is easy to read, including being easily readable on a mobile device. Use a basic font such as Arial, Tahoma, Verdana or Calibri. Use the same font throughout the résumé and be consistent in using bullet points or other formatting styles.

Having a well-crafted résumé can open the door to an interview and put you on the path to a job and a career. Writing a winning résumé takes time and planning. If you need help, there are many online tools and professionals that can help you, including RiseSharp, www.risesharp.com.

## Make Your Résumé Automation-Friendly

Companies of all sizes are now using automation to give résumés a first look. A software known as the applicant tracking system (ATS) ranks applications. To get past the automation, there are some things you need to know.

Make sure your résumé has the keywords that describe the skills needed for the internship. Don't stuff your résumé with keywords, but try to include them in your work experience and education sections. This can help advance the résumé beyond a robot and get the attention of the hiring manager or other decision maker.

## Show Your Personality

Because there may be many people applying for the job you're pursuing, you need to stand out from other applicants. Your cover letter, LinkedIn profile and any portfolio you are presenting need to show your skills and talents as well as your outstanding personal qualities and details about successes. This will add another dimension to your profile.

## Keep the Design Simple

Use a basic, simple design and format. Do not include any images. Images may make the ATS skip over it. If the instructions in the job listing ask for a PDF, then follow the directions. Otherwise do not submit a PDF, because the ATS may not capture it correctly. The best choice is to follow the employer's instructions.

## Don't Forget the Humans

Once your résumé gets past the ATS, it will be read by a person, so include all your information and have specifics related to the job you are applying to. Do not send the same résumé for all positions. Customize it for the position you are applying to. One way to do this is to revise the career objective section. Remember to use keywords that are included in the job listing.

## Sample Résumés

Having a good résumé is a basic requirement to be successful at job search. View a few sample résumés for various jobs.

# Sample Résumé for Entry Level Software Engineer Position

## Revathi Patil
+91-55555 55555          revathip@youremaildomainname.edu

**OBJECTIVE**
To use my strong coding and critical thinking skills to gain a position in software design and application development to drive product success in an agile environment

**EDUCATION**
**College of Delhi Technology,** New Delhi                    06/17-Present
BE in Computer Science
- Coursework has included Object-Oriented Programming, Introduction to SQL, Agile Software Development, Mobile App Programming, and XML
- **Captain, Women's Badminton Team:** Committed 20 hours per week to practice, both on the court & in the gym, to develop strength, technique and team coordination abilities
- **Teaching Assistant, Computer Science Department:** Supported faculty for Computer Science Lab courses, including conducting practice sessions and responding to student questions
- GPA: 3.7/4.0

**Gurgaon Valley High School,** Gurgoan                    07/14-04/17
- Research Project: Designed school yearbook using software tool, FlipBuilder
- Student Leadership Member, Badminton Team Co-Captain

**EXPERIENCE**
**New Tech Software,** San Francisco, CA                    Summer 2019
*Software Development Intern*
- Assisted the Director of Learning & Evaluation with the development of data sharing & coordination strategy projects to drive program improvements and outcomes
- Researched and presented findings on opportunities to improve re-usage of user interface elements
- Using R programming language and Excel created a user-friendly demographic dashboard that synthesized and visualized data across the various sites

**College of Delhi Technology,** New Delhi                    Summer 2018
*Campus Club Web Developer*
- Developed and launched website for campus club. Met regularly with the club's officers to establish goals for the website, including design and content specifications. Met all deadlines. Project was completed in 2 months.

**SKILLS & INTERESTS**
- Possesses strong oral and written communication abilities
- Member of Women in Technology and Social Justice groups
- Proficient in Java and R Programming Languages and MySQL Database
- Interests: Hiking, Reading, Classical Mythology

# Sample Résumé for Entry Level Finance Position

## Rajiv Singh
2424 Pearl Road, Hyderabad, TS 500100 | 555-555-5555 | rajiv.singh@youremaildomain.com

### SUMMARY
- Possess strong research, analytical, and communication abilities, with experience in financial statements
- Proficient in mathematics (statistics, probability, vector calculus, differential equations) and MS Office (Excel, PowerPoint, Word)

### EDUCATION
**College of Warangal**                                                    **Warangal, TS**
Bachelor of Arts in Statistics                                             Aug 2016 - May 2020
- Honors: Honors with Distinction (four semesters)
- Relevant Coursework: Financial Accounting, Linear Algebra/Differential Equations, Macro/Microeconomics, Calculus, Statistics
- Key Team Project: Developed a business plan, including 5-year financial projections, for a food delivery startup venture
- Activities: Warangal Investment Group, Cricket Club

**Hanamkonda Business Academy**                                            **Hanamkonda, TS**
Business Management Summer Program                                         Summer 2018
- The Hanamkonda Business Academy, a highly competitive program offered by the School of Business, provides an opportunity for talented college students to study business leadership and management

### WORK EXPERIENCE
**First Frontier One Solutions**                                           **Hyderabad, TS**
Financial Analyst (Intern)                                                 Summer 2019
- Created financial statements for an online venture focused on bringing technology-based design planning solutions to the mainstream architects
- Conducted market research to gather comparables' financial ratios, and performed analysis to validate assumptions
- Worked closely with VP of Marketing to understand the business model and to gather inputs

**Next Gen Peace Solutions International**                                 **Kazipet, TS**
Coach (Volunteer)                                                         Summer 2018
- Next Gen Peace Solutions International's mission is to unite, educate and inspire young people in divided communities through sports. NGPSI-Warangal strives to bridge gaps between children from different income levels
- Helped with planning and managing cricket practices, teamwork building exercises, and leadership conferences for 50+ kids, ages 10 to 16, from different parts of the state

**Tutoring**                                                              **Warangal, TS**
Tutor                                                                     2015 - Present
- Tutored mathematics subject, including variable calculus, to 10th grade and Intermediate students in the evenings and weekends

### EXTRACURRICULAR EXPERIENCE
**Warangal Cricket Club**                                                  **Warangal, TS**
Officer                                                                    2017 - 2018
- Responsible for coordinating events and recording weekly club meeting minutes for the 80+ member club

**Happy Life Microfunds**                                                  **Warangal, TS**
Co-Founder                                                                 2018 - 2019
- A high-school student run microfinancing initiative that promotes social entrepreneurship locally
- Recognized by the education minister in her annual education seminar, and featured in a newspaper

**Online Radio Station**                                                   **Warangal, TS**
Sports Broadcaster                                                        Sep 2016 - 2019
- Hosted a weekly sports talk show for three years – youngest on-air broadcaster
- Researched and analyzed national cricket stats to engage in on-air discussions with guests

# Sample Résumé for Entry Level Nursing Position

### Shree Savaar
Kochi, Kerala • shree.savaar@youremaildomainame.com • +91-55555-55555

## EDUCATION

**Kollam Technology & Medical University**　　　　　　　　　　　**Kollam, Kerala**
*School of Nursing, Diploma in General Nursing and Midwifery*　　　July 2018 - Current
Cumulative Marks: 86%

- Coursework included: Women and Infant Health, Psychology and Mental Health, Nursing Fundamentals, and Community and Environmental Nursing

- First Year Project: Developed and practiced patient history taking skills, at a local multi-specialty hospital, to improve the engagement with patients

## WORK EXPERIENCE

**Youth Apparel & Trends**　　　　　　　　　　　　　　　**Chennai, Tamil Nadu**
*Sales Assistant Intern*　　　　　　　　　　　　　　　　　Jun - Aug 2019
- Processed cash and credit transactions with customers
- Managed daily opening and closing procedures
- Assisted with store stocking and merchandising to maximize sales
- Filed and responded to any customer service complaints

## LEADERSHIP AND VOLUNTEER ACTIVITIES

**KTMU Student Residential Halls Committee**　　　　　　　　**Kollam, Kerala**
*Board Member*　　　　　　　　　　　　　　　　　　　　Aug 2018-May 2019
- Addressed housing/residential concerns from the student body
- Working with the administration, developed and passed residence hall regulations
- Created and maintained email database of residents
- Facilitated communication between students and staff to streamline facilities management
- Improved the overall resident satisfaction rating by 18%, to 87%, through expanded food service hours|
- Served as a liaison between the residence halls and the college's administration

**Kollam Regional Photography Club**　　　　　　　　　　**Kottarakkara, Kerala**
*Representative (Volunteer)*　　　　　　　　　　　　　　Aug 2019-Oct 2019
- Coordinated photography for all major social and cultural events in the district
- Hosted regional monthly photography contests
- Wrote stories for local newspapers

## ADDITIONAL INFORMATION

**Skills:** Proficient in Microsoft Office, Customer Care, Bookkeeping; Strong Communication Skills

**Interests:** Listening to Podcasts, Painting, Traveling, Blogging

*The Cover Letter*

## How to Write a Cover Letter

A cover letter is sent with your résumé and may be required. It is often an attachment or may be in the body of an email. It provides an opportunity to add information that's not in your résumé and explains how you are qualified for the job.

## What to Include in the Cover Letter

The cover letter should be divided into three parts:

* Introduction
* Body
* Closing

*Introduction*

The introduction states what position you are applying for. If there is someone in the company who referred you to the job, it's a good idea to mention that person.

*Body*

The body of the letter emphasizes relevant qualifications and experiences, and why you are a good fit for the job. This can be challenging if you don't have any job experience. It's important to look at the skills outlined in the job description and discuss how you've achieved any of these through your education, academics, on-campus or other experiences.

## Closing

The closing thanks the recipient for considering your information, sums up the contents of the letter and expresses that you look forward to talking with the employer about the position.

## Sample Cover Letters

Here is an example of a cover letter for a job in business:

Dear NAME,

I am applying for the internship with <name of company>. I learnt of the position through the training and placement office at <name of college>. I am very interested in this position, because I want to pursue a career in business.

I majored in entrepreneurship and business management, and received my degree on <add date>.

My goal is to work for a well-funded B2B start-up. I have read extensively about your company, and I believe this opportunity matches my career goals.

I understand you are seeking a candidate who is detail-oriented, has good communication and follow-through skills, and is also proficient in Microsoft Office and social media. In group projects, I was often the one who headed up the planning and execution, and made sure deadlines were met, including ensuring that the final project was submitted on time. My professors have had high praise for my follow-through, creativity and consistency. I am proficient in Microsoft Office and many of my business and marketing classes provided me with extensive knowledge of social media.

With my combined business and digital marketing knowledge, leadership skills and outgoing personality, I'm confident that I can meet your expectations and demands, and successfully develop my professional skills.

Thank you for considering my application. I look forward to having the opportunity to discuss my application with you at an interview. Please contact me at my phone number any time during business hours.

Sincerely,
Name
Phone number
Email
Link to website (if relevant)

Here is an example of a cover letter for a software engineer position:

Dear _____,

Please accept my résumé for the entry-level software engineer position.

I am a recent graduate of <name of college> with a degree in Computer Science. I have knowledge of several operating systems, software development tools, and networking and file systems. I also have practical experience having built websites for two on-campus clubs, which include features for students to register online for club events.

My experience also includes collaborating with students on class projects. I was often the one chosen to present our work. Putting together presentations improved my communication skills and being on a team improved my collaboration skills.

I believe my abilities and skills make me a good candidate for your company. I hope to have the opportunity to talk with you to share more about my work-related experiences. Thank you for your consideration. I look forward to hearing from you.

Sincerely,
Name

## *Creating a Great LinkedIn Profile*

Employers often look at applicants' LinkedIn profiles. To stand out, create a great profile that includes a strong summary and lists your skills, accomplishments and any awards you've received. Your LinkedIn profile provides an opportunity for you to sell yourself.

Here are some tips to create a LinkedIn profile that will set you apart from others:

## Have a Professional Photo

Your LinkedIn profile photo needs to be good quality so that you appear professional. Wear business-like attire, such as what you would wear to a job interview.

Do not use a photo of yourself at a party, cartoon avatars or with your pet, friends or family. For example, this is not a good choice for a profile photo:

The photo needs to be a headshot of you, dressed professionally and looking at the camera. This is a better choice for a profile photo:

## Add Information after Your Name

After your name, there's space for a few more characters. Add information about your career goals or area of study. Examples:

- Riya Patel ★ Recent Engineering Graduate
- Arjun Naveen ★ Recent Law School Graduate
- Hardeep Singh ★ Seeking a Career in Computer Science

## Write a Strong Headline

Under your name is the Headline section where there is space for a sentence. Write a description that will make an impact and provide information about what sets you apart from others, as well as highlighting your skills and what position you are seeking. Example: 'Recent graduate with honours seeking software engineering job.'

## Make Your Summary Stand Out

The Summary or 'About' section provides a lot of space for you to include more information about the type of position you are seeking, any experience you may have, including volunteer experience, descriptions of relevant projects you've worked on, your skills and how you can be an asset to a business or organization. Use keywords and phrases that are relevant to the industry you want to work in such as 'software engineer', 'graphic design', 'product marketing' or 'computer programmer'.

If you are unsure of what to include, search on LinkedIn for others who have the type of job you are looking for, such as 'staff accountant' or 'legal assistant' to see what they have included on their LinkedIn pages and model your page accordingly.

## Connect with Recruiters

LinkedIn has a section to let recruiters know that you are willing to be contacted by them. To find it go to the 'Jobs' tab in the main navigation and click on it. From there, you will see 'Career Interests'. Below that is a button you can turn on to let recruiters know that you are interested in being contacted.

## Accomplishments

If your GPA was 3.0 or higher, include it in your profile when seeking your first job. If you scored exceptionally well on state or national exams and you don't have a great deal of material to include in your summary, then consider listing your scores.

## Education

In the 'Education' section, list your education from secondary school through your college graduation. Include your major and any related programmes, such as study abroad.

*The Interview*

## Get Interview-ready

Before you walk into a job interview, it's important to be prepared. Be ready to answer questions and outshine the other candidates.

## Tips to Prepare for an Interview

Here are things to do in advance and during the interview to help you feel calm and confident:

1. Spend time **researching the company** you are applying to. Look for news items online and through LinkedIn as well as on the company's website, blog and social media sites. Being up to date on company news will reduce the chances that you'll be surprised

by any company information the interviewer discusses with you.

2.  If you're interviewing for a company that creates a product, try to use it, or at least get a **look at the product**, in order to be familiar with it before walking into your interview.

3.  Ask **who will be interviewing you**. Read their bios on the company website, if available, and look at their profiles on LinkedIn. You may see some things that you have in common to talk about at the interview. While it's okay to research those interviewing you, do not connect with them on LinkedIn until after you are offered the job.

4.  It's a good idea to ask about the company's **dress code**. For a company where the dress code is business casual, men might wear dress slacks, a button-down shirt and dress shoes. Women might wear light-coloured cotton clothing, or dress pants and dress shoes. For a company where the dress code is more formal, men and women should wear business suits.

5.  You have probably already sent your résumé when you applied for the job. However, it's a good idea to bring a copy with you in the event that the interviewer doesn't have one on hand. If you know that there will be more than one person interviewing you, bring a copy for each interviewer. Make sure your résumé is customized for the specific position you are applying for.

6.  If you are applying for a job, such as a graphic design position, where showcasing your work can

communicate your talents, bring your **portfolio**. For other jobs, you may want to bring **examples of work** to show your capabilities such as projects completed at college, awards, other professional recognition and any blogs or articles you have published on websites, in college publications or other media.

7. Try to **arrive a few minutes early**. Have directions to the location where the interview is being held and the phone number. If you are delayed, call to notify the interviewer that you are running late. You don't want to rush in late, be stressed out and have a poor interview.

8. The interviewer will be asking you questions to learn more about your skills, abilities and personality. Be prepared to **talk about achievements and experiences** at college, jobs or about instances where you have been successful. Show the interviewer that you have good judgement, take initiative, can work well on a team and have good leadership abilities.

9. One question you're likely to be asked is **why you are interested in the job** and why it's the right fit for you. In your answer, consider using some of the points from the job description. For a customer support job, you might say, 'Customer service is a good fit for me because I enjoy interacting with people, and I like being able to help people resolve their problems.'

10. In addition to answering questions, be prepared to **ask some questions**. Usually at the end of the interview, you'll be asked if you have any questions. Try to

avoid questions that can only elicit yes or no answers. Instead, ask thoughtful questions that show you have been researching the company and are interested in the job. Here are a few ideas of what to ask:

- **Can you explain what I will be doing on a day-to-day basis?** This question allows you to learn more about the position and any skills and abilities that are expected of you.
- **Can you describe a typical day?** This is similar to the above question, but it is more general, and makes it less about you.
- **What is the office culture?** Asking this question provides you with an understanding of whether you will feel comfortable and fit in well with the team.
- **What new job skills can I expect to acquire?** This shows that you are interested in growing within a specific industry.
- **What have you seen new hires do that has made them successful?** An answer to this question gives you insight into how you can be successful.
- **What are the next steps in the interview process?** By asking this question you are showing that you are interested in moving forward. The answer will provide you with information on whether you'll interview with additional decision makers and inform you of the hiring timeline.

11. If the **salary** was not listed in the job posting, be careful how you approach this. Often entry-level jobs do not have room to negotiate. If you put too much focus on your salary, then it might make the interviewer think that you are more interested in the money than the job. However, if possible, you should be knowledgeable about what the salary is, should the interviewer question you about how much you expect to be paid. Let the interviewer know that you are flexible regarding the salary so that you do not overvalue or undervalue yourself.

12. At the end of the interview, **ask for a business card** from each interviewer so that you have their contact information. Within twenty-four hours of the interview, or sooner if possible, email each interviewer a **thank-you note** expressing your appreciation for the interview. You can also reiterate why you want the job, your qualifications and how you are a good fit for the company. If you realize there was something you forgot to mention in the interview, you can include it in the thank-you letter. Keep it brief, and close the letter by saying that you look forward to hearing from them regarding the position.

## When you go to the interview, bring:

- Your résumé.
- Your portfolio (if applicable).

- A list of references—names and contact information of people who can speak positively about you such as professors, advisers or a former employer.
- A laptop, tablet or note pad and pen. (When the interview starts, ask if it's okay for you to take notes. This will help you to remember important points.)
- A list of questions to ask.
- Your photo ID to show proof of your identity.

## Common Interview Mistakes

Once you are invited to an interview, it's time to start preparing. Avoid the following mistakes that can cost you the job:

### *Don't Be Unprepared*

If you are unprepared, or don't show interest in the job and knowledge about the company, you might not be taken seriously. Research the company. By understanding its products, services and company culture, you will be able to intelligently contribute to the conversation, ask questions and provide information about how you might best fit in.

### *Don't be Unknowledgeable about the Company*

Research specifics about the company in advance of your interview. Here are three things that are helpful to know:

1. **Key team members**

   Look on the 'About' or 'Team' page of the company's website and read bios of key team members. If you can find out in advance who will be interviewing you, find information about that person on the website, Twitter or LinkedIn.

2. **Company news**

   Look at the company's 'News' or 'Blog' sections on their website, or their social media to understand its achievements.

3. **Clients**

   You should be able to find this information on the website. There might be a list of clients, case studies or project descriptions that will give you more insight about the company's work.

### Don't Arrive Late

Avoid being late by giving yourself plenty of time to get to the interview. Being late can make a bad first impression and lead the person interviewing you to believe that you have poor organizational skills. However, if something occurs, such as your train is late, or you are delayed in traffic, contact your interviewer to let him or her know what happened. This will show that you have a professional attitude.

### Don't Dress Inappropriately

One way to demonstrate that you will fit into the company's culture is by dressing appropriately and in a style similar to how the employees dress. Try to determine in advance whether people are wearing suits or are more casual. And what level of casual? Are they wearing T-shirts and jeans?

If the company has a casual dress code, this usually means a button-down shirt and nice pants for men, and pants and a nice top, or a cotton dress for women. For ideas for business casual dress, search for 'business casual attire for women' or 'business casual attire for men' on Google or Pinterest. If you are not sure what the company's dress code is, then it's best to dress more professionally than less.

### Don't Avoid Making Eye Contact with the Interviewer

When you meet the person interviewing you, make eye contact. This will help make a good impression and show that you are friendly and confident. Avoid looking down or focusing your gaze away from the interviewer. By looking at the interviewer, you are showing that you are prepared and ready to answer questions. Do your best to avoid appearing nervous or stressed.

### Don't Look at Your Phone

When you walk into the office where the interview is being held, turn your phone off and put it away. It is not acceptable to look at your phone, text, check the time or take notes on your phone during an interview. It is rude and inconsiderate. Give the interviewer your undivided attention. Taking notes is acceptable but use a pen and paper, or tablet.

## Don't Post on Social Media

Do not post on social media about your upcoming interview, and do not post information about what happened during the interview. The company may look at your social media and you do not want to say anything that can be misconstrued or hurt your chances for the job.

After the interview, do not ask the person who interviewed you to connect on LinkedIn or any social media.

## Don't Stretch the Truth or Lie

Answer all questions truthfully in the interview and make sure all information on your résumé is accurate. If you get caught being untruthful, you will be embarrassed, you won't get the job and you will hurt your reputation. If you don't tell the truth about your job skills and one of your references is called and doesn't verify what you've said in the interview or indicated on your résumé, it will have a negative effect. If you don't have some of the skills listed in the job description, it's acceptable to say that you are willing and interested to learn them.

## Preparing for Interview Questions

*Common Questions You'll be Asked in an Interview*

In preparing for an interview, it's helpful to have some idea of the type of questions you may be asked. While all interviews are different, here are some typical questions interviewers ask, as well as the purpose behind the questions and some suggested answers:

### Tell us about yourself.

The interviewer is looking for information that makes you a good fit for the job. It is not necessary to tell everything about your life. Instead, share a few things about some achievements in college, volunteer experiences or any work experiences you have had. Your answer should show the interviewer that you are a good learner and will do well in the position.

## What interests you about this job?

You want to show that you are enthusiastic about the position. Do not provide an answer such as, 'I need to get a job and noticed that you are hiring.' Instead, choose several key points from the job description and use those in your answer. Examples:

- *I am an excellent communicator and know that I would be good at customer service and support.*
- *I have built websites for several projects as well as for fellow students. I am confident that I have the skills to be a successful web developer.*
- *With my studies in accounting, along with my strong skills in math and excellent time management skills, I believe I can succeed as an accountant.*

## Why are you interested in a career in this industry?

Do some research before the interview to gain an understanding about the industry and to communicate why you would like to work in it. The interviewer may be trying to determine how knowledgeable you are about the industry and whether you are paying attention to related news and trends.

If you are applying for a job with a tech company, you may want to refer to a current trend if it's relevant to the conversation. An example might be talking about artificial intelligence (AI) and how it is changing technology.

Instead of making a general statement such as 'I find the industry very interesting,' talk about a specific innovation or trend you've been following, a leader in the field, or even someone at the company you're interviewing with. Talk about why you admire that person. Give specifics rather than generic statements. You can also talk about something related to the industry that you've learnt in your coursework, or on your own, and explain how it has provided you with additional industry knowledge.

Do not say that you do not know anything about the industry or ask the interviewer to explain it to you.

## What are your strengths?

An answer to this should be prepared in advance. Think about a problem that you were faced with, how you responded to it and the results. You could talk about a project in one of your classes that involved a team effort, or a situation you encountered in an internship or job. For example, perhaps you were on a team in which one member wasn't doing the work he was assigned. You could discuss how you approached that team member, the productive discussion you had and how you were able to get him to participate so that the project was successful. This would show that you have good leadership and communication skills.

## What are your weaknesses?

Prepare an answer to this question, but try to keep the answer positive even though the question is focused on a negative topic. Mention an area in which you need to grow, but talk about ways that you are working to improve.

For example, if you are likely to feel stressed when the workload becomes too heavy, suggested answers might be:

*A weakness I have is that I tend to feel stressed when there are a lot of projects to juggle. I work on managing it by making a list of what needs to be done and how to prioritize.*

*I sometimes have trouble determining how long it will take me to complete a project. To overcome this, I am taking an online class in time management skills.*

*I know that I need to improve my communication skills when I am making a presentation. I am working on this by spending extra time rehearsing before presentations.*

*I like to be in control. When working with a team, sometimes I will try to take over the tasks assigned to others. Some of this is because of my concern that everything will not get finished in time. To avoid this, it helps if, as a team, we can agree to create a list of everyone's tasks and have regular check-ins to be sure everyone is keeping to the timeline. This helps me avoid feeling anxious and taking control.*

## Don't Say:

* You are a perfectionist. It's something a lot of applicants say, and it will probably not be well received. People

may say it because they don't want to show that they have a weakness, but it's better to be able to show that you are aware of a skill or attribute that needs improvement.

- You have a weakness that is one of the main skills required for the job. Closely study the job description before preparing an answer.

## Tell us about a challenging or difficult situation you had to deal with and explain how you handled it.

This is another answer that you should be prepared for in advance. The question's purpose is to determine how you handle problems. Your answer should set up a scenario, so the interviewer understands what the situation was, the problem that occurred, how you tackled it and the results. Finish your answer with information about what you learned from the experience. If you do not have any work experience, you can refer to a difficult situation working with a team on a school project, or a situation you may have faced on your own. Example:

*I was heading up a team for a group school project and no one could agree on how to approach the project and create a timeline for it. I initiated a meeting and facilitated it so that everyone could listen to each other. I wrote down everyone's thoughts and identified where everyone agreed and disagreed. This allowed the group to create a streamlined approach and a timeline that everyone found to be workable. The lesson learned involved the importance of listening and learning to collaborate to get along as a team. By bringing the group together, I also improved my leadership skills.*

Often the interviewer won't leave the question open-ended, but will ask a specific question such as:

*How did you handle a difficult team member on a project?*
*How would you handle a difficult customer or client?*
*How would you handle a situation where you knew you were not going to be able to finish a project on time?*

Have answers to these and other behavioural-type questions prepared in advance to avoid being surprised. Remember to answer the questions by presenting:

- The problem
- The actions you took
- The result
- The lessons learned

## WORKSHEET: Notes to Prepare for Challenging Questions

Outlining your answers in advance will help you to be prepared and confident.

**Problem:**

_____

_____

**Actions I Implemented:**

_____

_____

**Lessons Learnt:**

_____

_____

**Problem:**

_____

_____

**Actions I Implemented:**

_____

_____

**Lessons Learnt:**

_____

_____

## Be Prepared for Unique Questions

Some interviewers ask unique and challenging questions. Examples:

- *What song would you sing in a televised voice competition?*
- *If you wrote a book about your life, what would the title be?*
- *If you were stranded in the desert and could only have three things, what would they be?*
- *If you could change something about yourself, what would it be?*
- *Talk about something that is not included on your résumé.*

The interviewer may be seeking to gain an understanding of your creativity and problem-solving abilities, and trying to determine your thought process, and whether you will fit into the company's culture. Be prepared to talk about more than what is included on your résumé.

If you are presented with a question that you don't have an immediate answer for, it's acceptable to pause and buy some time by saying, 'Well, that's a unique question; let me consider it for a minute.'

## Preparing for Different Types of Interviews

Your interview might not be in an office or a conference room. In fact, it might not be at the location of the business. Instead, it might be on the phone, Skype, a pre-recorded video interview, or in a coffee shop or restaurant.

*Phone Interview*

A phone interview gives an employer an opportunity to determine whether you fit the profile the company is looking for.

It might be scheduled in advance, but it's also possible that after you submit your application, you'll receive a phone call from the employer ready to talk with you at that moment about the position. Because of this, always sound professional when you answer the phone.

Here are six tips to prepare for either a scheduled or unscheduled phone interview:

1. You may have already researched the company before you submitted your application, but if not, take some time to become knowledgeable about it. Google the company, look at its website, read any relevant news articles as well as bios of the executive team and staff.

2. Have your résumé handy in the event you receive an unexpected phone call. Keep a copy on your desk, in your backpack and other places where you can quickly grab it regardless of where you are.

3. If the phone call is unscheduled, try to get to a quiet place as quickly as possible. If it's noisy, explain your situation. You can always ask if you can call the person back in five minutes, giving yourself time to get to a quiet location. If the call has been scheduled, be ready and in a quiet room.

4. For all mobile calls, be in a place with good reception. If the call is unscheduled and you do not have a good reception, move to another place as quickly as possible. Prepare for a scheduled call by being in a pre-selected location with excellent reception. You want the interviewer to be able to hear you and you want to avoid a dropped call.

5. Be prepared for the same types of questions that you would be asked in a face-to-face interview, including questions about your strengths, your weaknesses, why you want the job, your interest in the specific industry and answers to questions about specific scenarios, such as discussing a time when you succeeded as well as when you met with failure.

6. Have some questions ready to ask the interviewer. These can be the same as would be asked in a face-to-face interview such as what a typical day is like for someone in the position, the job skills that you'll gain and the most important qualities the company looks for in the job you're applying for.

## Mistakes to Avoid in a Phone Interview

Avoid the following three things and you'll have a good chance of being invited to a second interview, or even landing the job:

### 1. Sounding Unprofessional
Present yourself professionally. Be in a quiet place with no background noise or interruptions. Be in a

place with good cell phone reception and make sure your phone has a full battery.

2. **Being Unprepared**

   If you don't know anything about the company you are interviewing with, then your answers might not be relevant and the interviewer will know that you are not prepared. This could end your chances to land the job. Remember, there will be many candidates who will be prepared.

3. **Underselling Yourself**

   Highlight some of your achievements during the interview. Even if you have no job experience, you can talk about academic successes you've had, praise you've received from professors and any awards or honours you've earned. Do not hesitate to sell yourself as a good fit for the job.

*How to Prepare for a Pre-Recorded Video Interview*

Many companies and organizations will conduct an interview with you in person, but there are also employers who now conduct pre-recorded video job interviews. These are usually done early in the interview process and allow hiring managers to get a first impression of applicants. The interview will take place either at the company or at your own location.

The questions would be provided in advance and you are asked to record your answers within a specific amount of time. While this process may initially feel awkward, it allows you to prepare what you'll say in advance, giving you the opportunity to present yourself as a good candidate.

## Four Tips for a Successful Pre-recorded Video Interview:

1. *Pay Attention to Your Wardrobe*
   Wear the same type of clothing that you would wear if you were interviewing in person. In most cases this means business attire or business casual. Because you will be on camera, avoid wearing flashy prints or plaids. Stay away from clothing that is too light or too dark. If you wear a dark suit, wear a white or pastel shirt to create a good contrast.
2. *Dress for the Interview*
   Be professionally dressed from head to toe. Don't wear jeans with a business jacket and shirt or blouse. You don't want to be in a situation where you happen

to stand up during the interview and then it's revealed that you haven't taken care to dress for business.

3. *Be Aware of the Background*

   Be aware of the background and the lighting. The lighting should be above and in front of you so that it is on your face, and not at the back of your head. Sit in front of a blank wall or a background that is neat and orderly with no distractions. Practise in advance until you are comfortable and confident in the setting. Position the camera so it is not easy to identify objects behind you. If using a laptop, have it on a table or desk so that the image remains steady. Turn off your phone, and silence or remove any additional devices that might be distracting. Be in a quiet location where no one will enter the room.

4. *Prepare to Answer Questions*

   Although you can't see the person interviewing you, imagine someone sitting in front of you. If you are given the questions in advance, you can prepare your answers before recording the interview and spend time practising speaking the answers. Consider recording yourself, or ask a friend to listen to your responses. Ask them to provide input on how you can improve. While practice is helpful, try not to over-rehearse. You want to show your personality and have your voice sound natural.

   When recording your answers, look directly at the web camera rather than down at the computer screen. Try not to move around a lot because this can cause the images to be blurry. Don't shuffle papers, but keep a copy of your résumé, the job description, and other helpful notes in front of you for easy reference.

Often pre-recorded video interviews have a time limit. Put a clock where you can see it to stay within the allotted time frame.

*How to Prepare for a Skype or Zoom Interview*

The Skype or Zoom interview is a combination of a one-on-one interview and a phone interview. While you won't physically be in the interviewer's office, you will be visible on a computer or other screen, so pay attention to your physical appearance and the surrounding environment.

## Check Out the Company's Culture

Just as you would do for any other type of interview, research the company. Look at its website and social media sites. Try to gain an understanding of the company's culture and its people.

## Have a Professional Skype Presence

Have a professional Skype user name and photo. Try to choose a name that is firstname.lastname, or lastname.firstname. If your name is taken, use a middle initial or add a number at the end.

## Dress Professionally from Head to Toe

Although you are not in an office, dress as though you are. Dress professionally to match the company's culture. Dress nicely from head to toe, because even though you might be sitting behind a desk, if you make the mistake of standing up and have on jeans or sweats, you won't look professional.

## Create a Nice Setting

Be in a quiet room where you can shut the door. Make sure the background is professional. A blank wall or a well-organized bookcase or shelf is fine. Remove any personal items from the background. Inform everyone in your house not to enter the room where you are doing the interview. Close all programs on your computer. You don't want to be receiving Facebook notifications and other alerts during the interview.

## Conduct a Practice Interview

Ask a friend to talk with you on Skype and get feedback on how you look and sound. Make sure the audio and video are good. If you can record the practice interview, then you can review it and focus on any improvements that need to be made. Pay attention to looking at the camera and not down at the computer or screen.

## Handling Technical Difficulties

If there's a technical issue on your end, such as you lose sound or video, apologize, stop the call and call back, even if you have to end the Skype call and call by phone. As a result of this situation, the interviewer may realize that you are a quick thinker and can handle a problem.

If the technical issue is on the interviewer's end, bring the issue to his or her attention, and, if possible, politely suggest a solution.

## Send a Thank-you

Send a thank-you email after the interview. Thank the interviewer for his or her time and express your interest in the job. If you think of something that you forgot to mention, include it in the email.

## Get Hired Quickly

*Ten Tips to Help You Get Hired Quickly*

Applying for a job can be competitive and the stress of the search can be worrisome and hurt your confidence and self-esteem. However, there are a few things that can be done to reduce the stress. These ten tips are designed to improve your chances of quickly landing a job.

1. **Apply to Jobs Matching Your Skills**

   Spend your time wisely. Go after jobs that are the best fit for you. Focus on the positions you believe you would be good at, that you might have the skills for and are interested in. When looking at job postings, focus on the 'Responsibilities' section that describes what the job entails, and apply to those in which you can do some of what's listed, or are in an area that you are interested in pursuing. If you do not have all the qualifications, still consider applying. You can indicate in your cover letter that you believe you are able to learn the skills you don't currently possess.

   Focus your search and do not waste your time on those positions that are not a good match for you.

2. **Keep Applying**

   Even if you think you're a good match and have an excellent chance of being hired, don't stop applying. Continue to submit applications until you have an actual offer. Should you have more than one offer, you will be in a very good situation.

3. **Look for Companies Hiring Entry-Level Employees**

   Keep on the lookout for companies that regularly hire people right out of college. If a business has an ongoing need for new employees who are just starting out, this may increase your odds of getting hired.

4.  **Network to Get Inside the Company**

    All jobs are not found online. While online job sites are a good place to find employment, it's often possible to find a position by networking. Talk with others in the industry you're interested in pursuing, attend networking events, connect with people through LinkedIn, and let everyone know the type of job you are looking for. If you have friends who work at companies that are a good match for your skills, let them know you are interested in an internship or job. Sometimes knowing someone on the inside can be just the thing to help you land a position.

5.  **Revise Your Résumé to Match the Position**

    While most job hunters understand they need to write a separate cover letter for each job they apply to, it is also a good idea to tailor your résumé to each job. Review how the job posting is written and if you have some of the key qualifications listed, include them towards the top of your résumé. This can be time-consuming, but it may prove to be more successful than sending out generic résumés.

6.  **Have Someone Proofread Your Résumé**

    Before you send your résumé to a hiring manager, ask someone to proofread it. Even though you have worked very diligently to make it perfect, it's quite possible you may have a spelling error or have not included an important fact. Submitting a résumé without errors will show a potential employer that you pay attention to detail. A résumé filled with errors could cost you a job, and that's a mistake that can be avoided with the help of a proofreader.

7. **Dress for Success**

When you land an interview, you'll want to make a winning appearance. First impressions do matter, and studies show that hiring managers may take anywhere from a few seconds to several minutes to form an impression. Dress professionally based on the company and industry. If you are unsure about what to wear, a good rule is to dress one or two steps above the position for which you are applying. For example, if the position you're interviewing for is entry-level, then dress as though you are a manager. If you feel comfortable asking, inquire about the dress code when invited to an interview. That way, you have a good chance of showing up as someone who will fit into the company's culture.

8. **Prepare for the Interview**

Having your wardrobe planned out is just one step to prepare for a successful interview. In addition, once the interview has been scheduled, do the following:

- Research the company so you have some solid knowledge about what it does, some of its successes and basic information about the people who work there.
- Review the job description to refresh your memory on how your skills are a good match.
- Have your own success stories prepared about how your work, education or volunteer experiences relate to the position.

- Prepare questions to ask about the company.

9. **Ace the Interview**

   When the interviewer comes to the reception area to meet you, smile and be friendly, even if you have been made to wait a long time. Listen carefully to the questions and do your best to answer them conversationally, using your success story examples, where appropriate. If you don't know the answer to a question, be honest; but if it makes sense, you can explain that it's something you'd like to learn about, or perhaps consider asking a question related to what was asked. Do not try to be funny or make jokes. Your humour may not be the same as that of the interviewer. If the interviewer asks if you have any questions, ask the ones you've prepared if they haven't already been covered, or ask additional ones that you thought of during your interview. It's generally acceptable at the end of the interview to say that you are very interested in the position and ask when you can expect to receive a decision. Remember to thank the interviewer for his or her time.

10. **Write a Thank-you**

    Within twenty-four hours after an interview, send a thank-you note by email. Express your thanks for being considered for the job and once again state the fact that you are interested in the position. If there is important information that you forgot to mention during the interview, include it in the thank-you note. Keep the note short and proofread it closely or have someone else look at it to avoid any errors.

*Thank-you Note Examples*

## Sales Job

Dear <name of interviewer>,
Thank you for taking the time to interview me for the sales position. After speaking with you, I am very enthused about the possibility of working at your company and am confident that I would do a good job.

I will gladly answer any additional questions you may have. I look forward to hearing from you.

Sincerely,
Your Name
Phone Number

## Computer Science Job

Dear <name of interviewer>,
Thank you for providing the opportunity to interview with you. I enjoyed learning more about the position and the company's goals.

I am very interested in the job and feel that my education in business and computer science, along with my experience as an assistant in an IT Lab, will make me a good fit.

During my interview, I failed to mention that I had taken a class in data management and analysis. I believe the knowledge I gained in that class will help me to be successful.

I look forward to the next step in the application and interview process. Please feel free to contact me with any questions at <phone number>.

Sincerely,
Your Name
Phone Number

## Five Steps to Conducting a Strategic Job Search

Whether you are just starting to look for employment, or have been seeking a job for a while with no success, the problem might be that you don't have a job-search strategy. Putting a plan in place will help simplify the process and make it less stressful. Following these five steps will help you to be strategic and make the job search less overwhelming.

1. *Determine the type of job you want*
   Begin by developing a list of the kinds of jobs that interest you and that are based on your skills and talents. Take into consideration your college degree. If you have had any job experience through internships, temporary work or volunteer positions, consider what you liked or did not like at those jobs and any skills you acquired. Make a list of your skills and experience, and from this information, create a target list of the types of jobs and specific companies you want to pursue.

2. *Research the target companies*

   With the list you have created of target companies, spend time researching them. Be sure that you clearly understand each company's products or services. If a company has a news section or blog on its website, read through it to stay current on its thought leadership as well as any recent successes. On job posting sites, such as Naukri.com, look at what jobs are currently available, paying attention to the skills and experience they are looking for. To gain further insight, visit a website such as Glassdoor.com where you may be able to find reviews, salary information and, possibly, information about the hiring process.

3. *Create a résumé and cover letter to match your job search*

   Now that you know the types of jobs you are looking for and have gathered information about the skills and experience your target companies are seeking, you can create a résumé tailored to those businesses. Employers and hiring managers reportedly spend anywhere from only six to fifteen seconds reading a résumé before deciding whether it lands in the 'yes' or 'no' pile, so you need to grab their attention quickly. Along with highlighting your skills and experience, be sure to include keywords from the job description. This is especially important if the résumé is being screened by algorithms in ATS (Applicant Tracking System). For each job you apply to, write a cover letter customized for the skill set the employer is seeking.

4.  *Keep Your LinkedIn Profile Up-to-Date*

Be sure that you have a LinkedIn profile that's up-to-date and reflects your skills, experiences and job objectives. Include a professional photo. The headline below your name is what comes into view when people do a search so it should clearly communicate the type of job you're looking for and your skills. For example, 'Marketing pro for banking and finance', or 'Designer for digital media', or 'Seeking position as software development engineer'. Remain active on LinkedIn and showcase your area of expertise by posting updates, writing articles and being involved in groups. Make as many connections as you can. The more active you are, and the more connections you make, the more likely you are to be seen on LinkedIn.

5.  *Build Your Network*

In addition to building your online network, you'll also want to get away from your computer and meet people. Connect with friends, family contacts, acquaintances and friends of friends. Let them know what type of job you are looking for. Don't be afraid to ask for introductions to people at the companies you are targeting. You never know who may put you in contact with a decision maker who will make your dream job a reality!

## Five Dos and Don'ts for Writing Your Résumé

To create a strong, impactful résumé, you need to summarize your skills in a way that makes you stand out from the competition. The résumé is more than simply a list of your work experience, skills and the institutions you graduated from. It's important to present your career history and achievements in a way that will help you land an interview. Here are some dos and don'ts to create a stellar résumé .

*Dos*

1.  **Customize Your Résumé to the Job**
    Customize your résumé for each job you apply to. Be sure that your qualifications and skills match much of what is in the job description. Businesses often use an automated system to screen résumés for specific keywords so try to use some of the same phrases that are in the job post.

2.  **Use Numbers**
    When writing about your work experience, provide specific examples of how your work impacted the bottom line. Simply saying you did something, such as increased sales, is not as impressive as providing specific details. For example, instead of saying that you increased the company's sales, it will be more impressive and will better highlight your abilities to say that you increased company sales by 125 per cent. Or, instead of saying that you saved the company

money, be more specific with a statement such as, developed a new payroll system that saved the business INR 1 crore in personnel costs over a five-year period. Also, indicate if you were promoted or otherwise recognized for your achievements.

3. **Promote Your Tech Skills**

   If software and technology skills are mentioned in the job description, list those that you are skilled at, how long you've used each one and your level of proficiency.

4. **Inform References of Your Job Search**

   If you are starting on your job search and preparing to send out numerous résumés, it's a good idea to let the contacts who you will be using as references know that they may be getting a phone call or email. Provide them with a copy of your résumé so they are in the know about your work history and achievements and have the information to provide a good word about you.

5. **Ask a Friend to Proofread**

   You don't want to lose out on a job because you have typos or grammatical errors on your résumé. Proofread your résumé and ask a friend or a proofreading service to help. Those who are seeing the document for the first time are more likely than you are to catch errors and other mistakes.

*Don'ts*

1. **Don't Be Dishonest**

   Be truthful in all parts of your résumé. Do not be dishonest about where you've worked, the positions you've held or where you went to college. Lying can catch up with you and result in you not being considered for a position, or being fired if you land the job.

2. **Don't Explain Why You Left Previous Jobs**

   While it's important to list your past work experience and accomplishments, it's not necessary to explain on the résumé why you left a job.

3. **Don't Use Your Business Contact Information**

   When listing your contact information, do not have potential employers contact you at the phone number or email where you are currently working. Use your personal email address and phone number, even if you have told your current company that you are seeking another position.

4. **Don't Include Salary Information**

   If the job posting asks for a salary range or salary history, include it in the cover letter, unless it is specifically requested that it be included in the résumé. If the posting asks for your salary expectations, and you don't know what the salary is for the job you are applying to, it is often a good idea to include a salary range. This will allow you some flexibility and prevent you from asking for too low or too high a salary. To state a salary range that is reasonable, do some research to find information on what the average salary is for the type of position you are applying for. If a salary history or salary requirements are not requested, wait until your interview to discuss these topics.

5.  **Don't Create an Experimental Résumé Format**
    Creating a résumé with different colours and fonts
    will probably not prove effective. Hiring managers
    and recruiters want a résumé that's easy to read and
    that clearly communicates your work experience
    and skills. Stick with traditional résumé formats to
    improve the chances that your résumé will be read.

A well-written, professional résumé is the first impression
that a hiring manager has about you, so you want it to be
as near perfect as possible.

## How to Network to Find a Job After College

One way to jump-start your job search is to begin
networking. While it can be beneficial to reach out to
everyone you know and tell them what type of job you are
looking for, it's also important to build mutually supportive
relationships to generate job opportunities. Here are some
tips to help you with your networking efforts:

### Know Your Strengths and Skills

When looking for ways to network for an entry-level
job, it is important to identify your strengths, such as
critical thinking, problem-solving, time management,
technical, computer and administrative skills, and be
able to articulate why these are important for the types of
jobs you are seeking. Practise communicating real-world
examples of how you have demonstrated these skills at

college or in other situations and be able to share that information with those you are networking with.

## *Attend Events*

When you have established how you will present yourself, research business networking events to attend. These events, whether virtual or in person, will allow you to find opportunities and referrals. They can be a great way to begin looking for a job and build a referral network. You can find networking events by doing a Google search for 'business networking events' in the city where you are located.

If there are no networking events in your city, consider contacting fellow classmates and recent graduates, and create your own events to network with one another. Once you find an event to attend, try to find out which companies will be in attendance. Having this knowledge will let you do some research in advance on each company. This will help you to engage in a discussion about their businesses, as well as specific trends in their industries.

## *How to Introduce Yourself*

If you are talking with someone who works in an industry in which you would like to land a job, ask them about their business, what they are currently working on and what attracted them to the business they are in. It's acceptable to ask if the company currently has any openings, and what type of candidate they are seeking. If you believe you might be a good match for the job opening, share your skills and qualifications, and get information on how you might apply, but don't directly ask for a job.

Be sure to get contact information and business cards from those who you think may be able to help you. Perhaps, even suggest that you'd like to arrange a follow-up conversation sometime soon.

## Use Social Media

Use social media to reach out to people in companies where you're interested in working. Comment on their Twitter feeds and participate in LinkedIn groups they are members of. This is a great way to get noticed.

Whether networking through personal contacts, networking events or social media, remember that the purpose is to build your network of business contacts. This will increase the possibility of quickly landing a job that is a good fit for you.

## CHECKLIST: My Job-Search Readiness

Use this checklist to assess whether or not you are prepared to launch your job search.

☐ Identify and understand your personality type and interests.

☐ Research industries and career possibilities.

☐ Identify at least one specific career pathway that matches your personality and interests.

☐ Discuss career goals and aspirations with mentor, family and friends.

☐ Have a professional, updated résumé ready.

☐ Have a professional cover letter.

☐ Have a professional, updated LinkedIn profile.

☐ Have professional attire for interviews.

☐ Understand the importance of first impressions, from a friendly greeting to overall appearance.

☐ Practise interviewing in a mock set-up, responding to commonly asked questions.

**Notes:**

_____

_____

_____

_____

_____

_____

_____

_____

_____

_____

_____

_____

_____

*'If you're offered a seat on a rocket ship, don't ask what seat! Just get on.'*

—Sheryl Sandberg

# PART IV

# THE IMPORTANCE OF A MENTOR

'*As we look ahead into the next century, leaders will be those who empower others.*'

—Bill Gates

## Finding a Mentor Who Is Right for You

Finding a mentor can be a solid building block for getting an internship or job and is also extremely beneficial as you move forward in your life and career. A good mentor will help you grow and succeed in your career.

*How to Find a Mentor*

In your first year of college, your college may assign you a professor as your mentor. If your school does not have a mentorship programme, or you have already graduated, you can find a mentor by asking for recommendations from professors, graduates of your college who are in a career that you want to pursue, or other friends and family.

Your placement office can help you with the following:

- Clarifying your academic and professional goals
- Developing your résumé
- Establishing a professional online presence
- Researching companies and job roles
- Sharing interviewing strategies, tips and best practices
- Increasing your confidence and motivation

> *'Choose a master whose life, conversation and soul-expressing face have satisfied you . . . For we must indeed have someone according to whom we may regulate our characters; you can never straighten that which is crooked unless you use a ruler.'*

> —Seneca the Younger (Stoic philosopher)

## Schedule a Meeting with a Potential Mentor

When seeking a mentor in the business world, don't simply call or email someone and ask them to be your mentor. Schedule an informational meeting to learn about them and their work. The meeting does not have to be at their office. It can be a meeting over coffee, or on Zoom that can last anywhere from thirty minutes to an hour.

As an advisee, you should:

- Bring your questions and reflections on what has and what has not been working for you.
- Be open and honest with your adviser about your interests, concerns and challenges.
- Remain open to a career adviser's feedback and suggestions.

- Keep your appointments.
- Notify in a timely manner if you need to reschedule.

## Ask Questions

During the meeting, take time to learn about the potential mentor's background and work. Ask basic questions such as:

- What do you do in your job?
- What is a typical day like in your job?
- What is your background (education, work experience) that led to you choosing your career?
- What is the industry outlook for the type of work you do and the industry you work in?

## After the Meeting

After the meeting, evaluate how you felt about the person. Is he or she someone that you would feel comfortable spending time with? Did you feel that you could have a good connection with this person? Did the person ask you questions and seem interested in what you had to say? Ask yourself some of the following questions to help determine if the person is the best fit for you.

### *Do I Admire This Person?*

Is this a person whose successes and experience are admirable to you? Has this person achieved things that you hope to accomplish someday?

## *Does This Person Like Their Job?*

Just because someone is successful in their job, it doesn't always mean that they enjoy what they do. If the person you're considering as a mentor is unhappy in their job, they may not inspire you. Find someone who enjoys their work.

## *Does This Person Have Good Contacts?*

Getting introduced to others in the field can create new opportunities. Ask your potential mentor if they have good contacts in the industry and discuss the likelihood of them being able to make introductions for you.

## *Can I Communicate Well with This Person?*

While a potential mentor may have industry experience and successes, be sure that the person is someone you can communicate with. Ask yourself:

- Is the person going to be easy to talk to?
- Will they be able to communicate what's needed to help you grow in your career?
- Will the person's style of communication be able to motivate and inspire you?
- Will they be able to communicate the knowledge you need to advance in your industry?

If you hesitate to answer yes to many of these questions, then it may not be a good match, so keep looking.

*Send a Thank-you*

Send an email thanking the person for taking the time to meet you. If you feel the person could be a good mentor for you, ask for another meeting. It is a good idea to establish a business relationship before creating a mentoring relationship.

## Tips for Finding a Mentor

- Don't ask the CEO of a company to be your mentor. During the time you are preparing to enter the workforce, ask for someone who has several years of experience, but not necessarily the top executive.
- Think about the information that will be most valuable to you, such as how to get started in your desired career and choose someone who can provide that knowledge.

## Your Relationship with Your Mentor

*What to Say When You Ask the Question*

When you are ready to ask someone to be your mentor, don't simply say, 'Will you be my mentor?' Instead, consider saying something such as, 'I appreciate your knowledge about this industry and would welcome the opportunity to continue to learn from you. Would you be willing to mentor me?'

*Define the Relationship with Your Mentor*

Be specific with your mentor about what you are looking for in the relationship. Be clear about what you hope to gain. How much time do you expect you'll need from your mentor? Will you need to talk with them one hour a month or more? Will you meet over the phone or coffee or lunch? What topics do you think you'll be discussing? Will you be asking for advice about your career? Will you be asking them for job opening information or people you can meet? Being clear in the beginning about what you are looking for will help you and the mentor have a successful relationship.

*Building a Working Relationship with Your Mentor*

Once you find someone who will be a good mentor, it's time to get started on building a successful working relationship. Here are some ideas to best use your time with your mentor.

*Rely on Your Mentor's Contacts and Knowledge*

Ask your mentor to help you take the first steps in your career by assisting you in areas that may include improving your résumé and making introductions to those who can be influential in your growth. Rely on your mentor's knowledge about trends in your industry and the steps you need to take to grow.

## *Be Considerate of Your Mentor's Time*

Work out a schedule with your mentor so they are able to devote time that works for both of you. Before establishing a schedule, think about whether you will need the person to meet with you twice a month, once a month, or more or less.

## *Discuss How the Mentor will Help You Achieve Your Goals*

Discuss with your mentor that you want to develop a plan that holds you accountable for tasks and goals that will help you to move in a positive direction. This will also help you to develop practices that will prove successful in the workplace. Be sure to hold up your end of the bargain and complete what's assigned to you.

# PART V

# CAREER PLANNING AND CHECKLIST

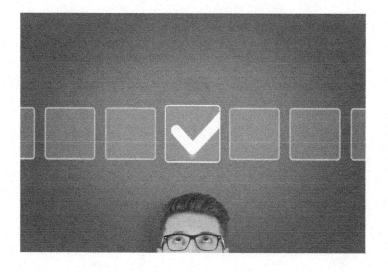

'You are capable of more than you know. Choose a goal that seems right for you and strive to be the best, however hard the path. Aim high. Behave honourably. Prepare to be alone at times, and to endure failure. Persist! The world needs all you can give.'

—E.O. Wilson

## Begin Career Planning Early

Early career planning can help you jump-start your journey from college to career. Putting a plan in place will help simplify the process and make it less stressful. Career planning begins with self-discovery. Career planning and development is an ongoing process that helps you discover who you are and what is most important to you in your life and work.

- The first step in exploring your career options is to gain a solid understanding of your interests, skills and knowledge. Identify your strengths and interests by completing self-assessments. When it comes to planning your career, there are many pathways available to you.
- Discuss your career aspirations and possibilities with career advisers, family, faculty and industry professionals. Research companies and roles that interest you. Conduct informational interviews with family contacts, alumni or industry professionals to further clarify your interests.
- Attend career fairs and networking events to learn more about opportunities and talk with employers about your abilities and skills. These events provide

a great opportunity to practise and refine your elevator pitch about your career goals, education and experience.

- Create a résumé and cover letter highlighting your career goals, strengths, skills and accomplishments.
- Build your professional network by connecting with faculty, alumni, industry professionals and employers, and talking with them about your interests. Also, create or update your LinkedIn profile and connect with peers and professionals in your industry.
- While in college, gain exposure and experience, and develop your interests, skills and strengths by engaging in extracurricular activities, volunteer opportunities and leadership positions. Seek out part-time work and internships.
- Research organizations of interest to learn about their mission, vision, values and company culture.
- Launch your job search. Explore full-time job opportunities related to your field of interest through career fairs, your network and online job boards.

## Career Planning Checklist

This checklist is your general guide to help you plan your career and successfully execute your job search. The earlier you start, the better you will be prepared. While in college, develop your interests, skills and network by engaging in extracurricular activities, internships and volunteer opportunities.

| Area of Focus | Description |
|---|---|
| **Academic Performance** | Your grades will be important to finding an internship or job. Focus on your academic performance. Develop the ability to effectively manage your time, commitments and relationships to reduce stress and perform well. |
| **Faculty Relationships** | As you progress through your college education, build relationships with your professors and teachers. Set a goal to get to know at least one professor well each year. Building this relationship will become handy when you need recommendation letters or career advice. |
| **Extracurricular Activities** | Depending upon your interests, get involved on campus in at least one extracurricular activity (e.g., sport, club). These can help you build your résumé, while further developing your interests and passions. |
| **Access Resources** | Review how-to guides and take self-assessments to help you gain skills and confidence to embark on a successful job search and career. |

| Area of Focus | Description |
|---|---|
| **Gain Experience** | Acquire experience during the breaks through volunteering, part-time work, research work and internships. It is important to gain experience and build critical employability skills while in college. |
| **Develop Résumé and Cover Letter** | Develop your résumé and cover letter to highlight your experience and skills. Continue to update your résumé with each new experience. Make sure to ask at least two people to review your résumé and cover letter. |
| **Talk to Industry Contacts** | Connect with your direct and indirect contacts in the industry (family, friends, alumni, faculty) to learn more about your industry of choice and fine-tune your job search strategies. |
| **Mock Interviews** | Prepare for interviews by practising mock interviews. Develop a list of standard questions and responses. |

'*The future depends on what you do today.*'

—Mahatma Gandhi

# PART VI

# CAREER PATHWAY

*'Whatever you decide to do, make sure it makes you happy.'*

—Paulo Coelho

## Career Pathway

The following is a recommended multi-year plan and timeline to get job ready and to transition from college to career successfully.

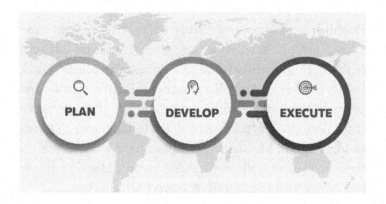

*PLAN*

## Be Successful in College

Develop strong academic habits from the beginning. Maintaining a strong GPA will help you gain access to the greatest number of job opportunities, from internships to full-time positions. Give proper focus to your academic performance. Develop an ability to effectively manage your time, commitments and relationships to reduce stress and perform well. If you are struggling to adjust to college academics, don't hesitate to seek out help from faculty, a mentor or administration. Jump-start your journey to a career through a well-developed plan. Early career planning can help you break into the job of your choice. The key to having a job when you graduate is to begin preparing as early as possible.

## Establish a Professional Email Address

Establish a professional email address with your first name and/or last name or some variation thereof (e.g., FirstInitialLastName, FirstName.LastName, FirstNameMiddleInitialLastName). Emails with just a few letters and numbers (e.g., rajj-rao1974@yahoo.com) don't look as professional as a full name in an email address. AOL, Hotmail and Yahoo have a dated feel to them. Use your college-provided email address or create one with gmail.com, outlook.com or icloud.com.

## Review Your Social Media Presence

Review your social media presence (e.g., Facebook, LinkedIn) to remove any inappropriate content or make any such content private. Social media is playing a role in how employers evaluate job candidates. Some employers tend to review candidates' social profiles before offering a job.

In a competitive job market, you need to present yourself well in person, on your résumé and online. Avoid posting (or participating in) inappropriate or offensive comments or photos online. Present a friendly, caring and professional profile (e.g., upload a professional photo to your LinkedIn profile; associate yourself with social causes).

## Take Self-Assessments

The first step in exploring your career options is to gain a solid understanding of your interests, skills and knowledge. Identify your strengths and interests by completing self-assessments.

Take self-assessments (Personality Assessment, Interests Assessment, Values Assessment, Skills Assessment) to gain a better understanding of yourself. Identify your career interests, values, skills and personality traits.

## Obtain a Professional Wardrobe

Obtain a professional wardrobe for informational interviews, job interviews, internships and career fairs. Speak to your placement office or mentor if you have any questions on the type of professional attire appropriate for your field. Your professional appearance (neat and clean) can make a great first impression.

## *DEVELOP*

## Develop Skills and Competencies

While in college, develop skills and competencies sought by employers, from communication to teamwork, through experiential learning opportunities. Gain experience through academic projects, internships, extracurricular activities, family responsibilities and/or volunteer positions.

## Attend Career Fairs and Events

Attend career fairs and other career recruiting events on campus and off campus. These events offer you great opportunities to meet and network with employers and learn about industry trends.

Career fairs and networking events offer opportunities to talk with employers about your abilities and skills. These events provide a great opportunity to practise and refine your elevator pitch about your career goals, education and experience.

## Build Your Professional Network

Build your professional network of contacts, including those made through job shadowing, internships, volunteering and informational interviews.

## Create or Update Your Résumé

Create your résumé using Résumé Builder, available to you through RiseSharp, a career services site, and through your placement office. Continue to update and polish your résumé for your target jobs by highlighting your career goals, strengths, skills and accomplishments. Ask at least two people to review your résumé for any spelling or grammatical errors.

## Establish a LinkedIn Profile

Establish a LinkedIn profile. If you already have one, keep it updated. Your LinkedIn profile can help you to establish professional connections, and explore and find job opportunities. Your LinkedIn profile is your online résumé.

Here are some general tips on how to create a powerful LinkedIn profile:

- Upload a professional-looking photo for the profile picture.
- Add a headline—a great way to pull a reader in.
- LinkedIn allows you to customize your public URL. Try to include your name in the URL.
- Remember to make your profile public, so others can find and access it.
- Make sure to add past experiences, projects, activities, awards and achievements.

## Participate in Clubs or Extracurricular Activities

Explore and participate in on campus or off campus clubs or extracurricular activities that are based on your interests. Your participation in extracurricular activities can help build your résumé and land an internship or job in the future.

You can also enhance your résumé with your academic work and on-campus positions. Examples:

- **Academic Experiences**
  Case studies, class projects, field trips, dissertations, guest speakers, research projects, academic competitions, group volunteer initiatives

- **On-Campus Experiences**
  Research assistant, teaching assistant, peer tutor, residential hall adviser, campus ambassador, lab assistant, library assistant

- **Extracurricular Experiences**
  Student government, visual and performing arts, community service, academic clubs, professional clubs, sports clubs, hobbies and special interests, media, religious interests, recreation and fitness, volunteerism

- **External Experiences**
  Job shadowing, internship, part-time job, volunteer service, full-time job, extracurricular activities, family responsibilities

These experiences can help you demonstrate your dedication, teamwork, time management, digital competence, communication skills and confidence. An experience can make you attractive to potential employers!

## Research the Jobs that Interest You

Research the jobs that are of interest to you. Find two to three such jobs and look at the skills required. Identify technical and domain competencies required for your dream job and create a plan to develop the required technical skills. It will give you a good understanding of the skills you may require to develop domain competency.

## Develop a Cover Letter

Develop a cover letter for your target jobs and have it reviewed by two or three people (e.g., placement staff, mentor, family friend). Your cover letter should highlight your career goals, strengths, skills and accomplishments.

The cover letter complements your résumé and is usually sent in the body of an email or as an attachment. It provides an opportunity to add to your résumé and explains how you are qualified for the job.

## *EXECUTE*

## Participate in Informational Interviews and/or Job Shadowing

Seek and participate in informational interviews and job shadowing, and talk to people working in jobs that interest you. These can help you learn more about your chosen career path and help you prepare for interviews by empowering you with a wealth of information to answer commonly asked interview questions.

## Evaluate Job Offers

Weigh the pros and cons of your job options before you accept any offer. Discuss it with your placement office, mentor and friends/family to get guidance.

## Going for Further Studies?

If you're considering going for further studies (e.g., graduate education), learn about your options and the entrance requirements (e.g., entrance exam).

## Launch Your Job Search

Find and apply to jobs related to your field of interest through career fairs, your network, on-campus job boards and online job boards. Searching for a job requires a plan and takes time. Try to take advantage of all the resources that are available to you through RiseSharp, a career services site, and through your placement office.

## Participate in Mock Interviews

Participate in mock interviews. The more interview practice you have, the more confident and successful you will be. Your placement office, mentor, professors and professional contacts can help you prepare for interviews. Review and practise commonly asked interview questions (e.g., 'Tell me about yourself'). Interview practice helps you land your dream job.

## Request Recommendation Letters

Identify and request recommendation letters from at least three references (e.g., your professors, your managers at work outside of college, a supervisor or manager from an internship).

## Meet with Your Placement Office

Schedule a meeting with your placement office to discuss your career goals, and to discuss experiential learning and internship opportunities. Your placement office can help you develop an action plan and achieve your career goals.

## Update your Outcome Status

Update your placement office with your final outcome status.

## Don't Have a Full-Time Offer Yet?

If you don't have a full-time job offer by now, accelerate your job search. Identify and address any gaps in your preparation. Expand your job search criteria by working closely with your placement office and mentor.

Sometimes, getting a job doesn't go as well as planned. Make sure to find out why you may be having trouble securing a job. Seek guidance and help from your placement office, mentor, or family or friends. Common reasons for not getting a job can be:

- Lack of preparation—from developing a résumé to preparing for an interview.
- Not being motivated—lack of motivation or passion can easily derail anyone's job search.
- Unrealistic expectations.

*'One important key to success is self-confidence. An important key to self-confidence is preparation.'*

—Arthur Ashe

# PART VII

# SELF-ASSESSMENTS

'*Self-analysis requires reconsideration of who we think we are. Self-awareness requires us to reassess where we came from and where we are going.*'

—Kilroy J. Oldster

Self-assessments can help you understand and articulate the environment and situations where you can leverage your strengths to thrive. This process helps you stay involved and motivated in planning and developing your career.

By spending time taking the assessments on the following pages, you will gain information about who you are—your personality, your behaviour in various situations, how you think, and areas of value and importance to you. This information will cause you to better understand yourself and can help you gain insight into the types of jobs and working environments that may be a good fit for you. For example, if your answer to whether you enjoy working in a team environment is 'strongly disagree', then you should not apply to jobs that involve teamwork and collaboration. Instead, you may be better suited to a job such as an accountant, a medical technician, or a market research analyst—jobs where you are not consistently involved with a team.

Once you have gone through the assessments, review them with a family member, professor or mentor—someone who can provide insight into whether your answers are a true picture of your qualities and characteristics, and how these may impact the types of jobs where you are likely to be successful.

Your answers may also be helpful when preparing for an interview. They can be a foundation for answers to questions such as 'Tell me about yourself', or 'What are your interests?' By discussing your attributes with potential employers, they will get a clear understanding of whether your personality, values, preferred work environment and competencies will make you a good fit for the position you are interviewing for.

## Personality Assessment

Personality is unique to each individual and it includes habits and traits acquired over the years. The personality test is designed to find out what you are like as a person and your work-related personality. Understanding your personality can help you to articulate the environment and situations where you can leverage your strengths to thrive.

Please rate your agreement or disagreement with the following statements:

### I enjoy making detailed plans:
o   Strongly agree
o   Agree
o   Neutral
o   Disagree
o   Strongly disagree

### I have clear goals:
o   Strongly agree
o   Agree
o   Neutral

o  Disagree
o  Strongly disagree

**I like everyone I meet:**
o  Strongly agree
o  Agree
o  Neutral
o  Disagree
o  Strongly disagree

**I prefer to finish tasks quickly rather than perfectly:**
o  Strongly agree
o  Agree
o  Neutral
o  Disagree
o  Strongly disagree

**Money motivates and energizes me:**
o  Strongly agree
o  Agree
o  Neutral
o  Disagree
o  Strongly disagree

**I enjoy working in a team environment:**
o  Strongly agree
o  Agree
o  Neutral
o  Disagree
o  Strongly disagree

## Interests Assessment

Interests can include hobbies, passions and curiosities. You can use your interests to identify careers of interest, and your career can evolve to support your interests and develop new interests. The Holland Codes or the Holland Occupational Themes (RIASEC: Realistic, Investigative, Artistic, Social, Enterprising, and Conventional) refer to a theory of careers and vocational choices (based upon personality types) that was developed by American psychologist John L. Holland.

Provide separate rankings for each interest. For example, you cannot rank both *Realistic* and *Investigative* interests #4. Each item must have a separate ranking.

| Interest | Description | Rank 1–6 (1–agree the least; 6–agree the most) |
|---|---|---|
| Realistic (Practical) | Enjoy practical and physical. Engage with tools, machines and gadgets. | |
| Investigative (Analytical) | Enjoy gathering information and conducting analysis. Appreciate intellectual activities and tasks. | |
| Artistic (Creative) | Enjoy aesthetics and self-expression. Favour unstructured environments. | |

| Interest | Description | Rank 1–6 (1–agree the least; 6–agree the most) |
|---|---|---|
| Social (Connected) | Enjoy helping, training and counselling. Thrive on engaging with others. | |
| Enterprising (Influential) | Enjoy managing and persuasion. Prefer to lead. | |
| Conventional (Systematic) | Enjoy details and accuracy. Comfortable with structure and within a chain of command. | |

## Values Assessment

Your values are the principles that are important to you and by which you live your life. Rank each value, thinking about how important the value is to you in a work setting.

Check a box corresponding to each of the following values on a scale from 1 to 5.

1: Not at all important
2: Slightly important
3: Important
4: Fairly important
5: Most important

|                            | 1 | 2 | 3 | 4 | 5 |
|----------------------------|---|---|---|---|---|
| Fun                        |   |   |   |   |   |
| Job                        |   |   |   |   |   |
| Recognition                |   |   |   |   |   |
| Compensation               |   |   |   |   |   |
| Loyalty                    |   |   |   |   |   |
| Structure                  |   |   |   |   |   |
| Independence               |   |   |   |   |   |
| Respect                    |   |   |   |   |   |
| Risk-taking                |   |   |   |   |   |
| Variety                    |   |   |   |   |   |
| Learning                   |   |   |   |   |   |
| Training and Development   |   |   |   |   |   |
| Colleague Relationships    |   |   |   |   |   |
| Making a Difference        |   |   |   |   |   |
| Creative Opportunities     |   |   |   |   |   |

## Employability Skills Assessment

Assess your professional skills and competencies that need to be developed to be career ready. Ask your placement officer or mentor to assess your employability skills.

*Teamwork*

Assess yourself: I build and maintain collaborative relationships to work effectively with others in a team setting through shared responsibility and respect. I have the ability to manage my emotions and tactfully handle conflict with others while contributing towards a common goal.

o   Excellent ability
o   Developing
o   Need to develop
o   Not required

## Ways to improve this competency include:

- Collaborate with others on a project where responsibility is shared (not divided).
- Prepare to handle challenging conversations in person without raising your voice or losing your cool.
- Consider the thoughts and perspectives of others before making a decision or coming to a conclusion.
- Engage in conversation with individuals who have different perspectives than your own.
- Take on additional responsibilities by going beyond your standard job description.
- Attend an event or gathering that encourages you to step outside your comfort zone and broaden your horizons.

**Here is my plan to develop my teamwork competency:**

_____

_____

_____

_____

_____

_____

_____

*Communication*

Assess yourself: I articulate thoughts and express ideas effectively using oral, written and non-verbal communication skills, and I am a good listener. I have the ability to successfully deliver information in person, in writing, and through digital means.

- Excellent ability
- Developing
- Need to develop
- Not required

**Ways to improve this competency include:**

- Develop and deliver a presentation to a group.
- Practise asking qualifying questions when conversing with others.
- Proofread online and written communications to improve communications and avoid errors.

**Here is my plan to develop my communication competency:**

_____

_____

_____

_____

_____

_____

_____

_____

_____

_____

_____

_____

*Problem-Solving and Critical Thinking*

Assess yourself: I exercise sound reasoning to analyse issues, synthesize information, make decisions and solve problems. I have the ability to think critically and creatively to develop original ideas and innovative solutions.

- Excellent ability
- Developing
- Need to develop
- Not required

**Ways to improve this competency include:**

- Build an action plan with specific steps to solve a problem.
- Brainstorm solutions to a problem with a project team.

**Here is my plan to develop my problem-solving and critical thinking competency:**

_____

_____

_____

_____

_____

_____

_____

_____

_____

*Professionalism and Work Ethic*

Assess yourself: I demonstrate integrity, accountability and ethical behaviour. I have the ability to maintain effective work habits to produce high-quality work and project a professional presence.

- Excellent ability
- Developing
- Need to develop
- Not required

## Ways to improve this competency include:

- Plan and prioritize work assignments and meet deadlines.
- Reflect on any recent challenge and identify areas of growth and improvement.
- Respond positively to change proposals and practices.
- Practise to motivate team members with a positive attitude to achieve common good.
- Look at your online presence and participation through the eyes of an employer and determine appropriateness.

## Here is my plan to develop my professionalism and work ethic competency:

_____

_____

_____

*Digital Competence*

Assess yourself: I have the knowledge and skills to use a range of common digital systems, technologies and applications for information-gathering, communication and problem-solving related to job tasks and projects. I have the willingness to continually update my digital abilities.

- Excellent ability
- Developing

- Need to develop
- Not required

## Ways to improve this competency include:

- Self-directed learning of most commonly used digital business applications (e.g., Microsoft Office).
- Communicate with internal and external constituents using an email application (e.g., Microsoft Outlook, Gmail).
- Learn and adapt new technologies to improve productivity and results.
- Develop academic project documents with graphs, using Microsoft PowerPoint or Google Slides.

## Here is my plan to develop my digital competency:

_____

_____

_____

*'We just need to remove the blinders from our eyes to have a neutral, level-headed and logical viewpoint based on self-evaluation.'*

—Dr Prem Jagyasi

# PART VIII

# STRATEGIES TO GET JOB READY DURING A PANDEMIC OR AN ECONOMIC DOWNTURN

Shortly after this book was written and submitted for publication, India, along with the rest of the world, was impacted by the COVID-19 pandemic. It's unknown whether this virus will be with us for many years, or whether in the future we will experience another pandemic or economic downturn from this, or another virus or event.

Although the COVID-19 pandemic caused the world to shut down, and future pandemics (should they occur) may do the same, it does not mean that you need to shut down the work required to get job ready. In fact, choosing to not do anything can have a negative impact. It can slow down your job search, and put you in the slow lane in the competitive race to land a job.

While many businesses may stop hiring as they determine how to move forward, they will eventually resume hiring and onboarding new employees. Implementing the following tips and strategies will help keep you on the path to successfully transitioning from college to career.

## Keep Your Résumé Up to Date

If you have not yet completed your résumé, now is the time to finish writing it so that it can be sent out for current job openings or when opportunities are available that you are a good candidate for. Look at online job sites as well as companies you are interested in working for to determine if there are jobs you want to apply to. Revise your résumé so that it is customized for each job you are applying to, or plan to apply to. Label each résumé in your files, making it clear what type of job it is suitable for, so when similar jobs open up you can easily access the résumé, quickly make any necessary edits, and send it out.

## Write or Update your LinkedIn Profile

Devote time to writing your LinkedIn profile. Or, if you have already written one, make sure it is up to date. Take a closer look to make sure you are highlighting your accomplishments. Were you an officer in a club? Did you have a lead role in a class project? If you are having trouble defining what qualities are related to some of your accomplishments, ask club members or those with whom you worked on a project to talk with you about how they viewed your participation or leadership. Some of what they discuss with you might be useful to use on your LinkedIn profile.

Recommendations help you stand out from the competition. Ask a professor, coach or other person that you have had a professional relationship with to write a recommendation for you. Let them know that a few sentences highlighting your achievements and/or qualities such as work ethic is all that is needed. You can even provide some bullet points to help them recall some of the work or tasks you were involved with.

Does your profile photo need improvement? Ask someone to take a good-quality photo of you with a neutral background that shows you in a professional light.

Join LinkedIn groups that are relevant to the industry sector you want to work in. Reach out to members of groups and ask them about job openings or for introductions to those you'd like to network with. Ask about virtual networking meetings where you can begin to build professional relationships.

## Continue Extracurricular Activities

Are you in a leadership position at a club or team at school? Continue running the club via online tools such as video conferencing (e.g., Zoom, WebEx, Google Meet). This will allow you to continue to promote the club's accomplishments in your job applications and interviews, and will help you continue to improve your leadership skills. If you are on a sports team, suggest to teammates that you can lead workouts virtually. This will keep you in shape and show potential employers that you are creative and take initiative. You can also explore opportunities to volunteer, virtually or in person (e.g., raise funding for social causes, help out those who are most vulnerable, be a caregiver or tutor online). Studies show that those who volunteer report having higher levels of happiness.

## Practise for Interviews

Review the commonly asked interview questions in Part III and practise answering them. You can role-play with a friend or family member. This may help you be more relaxed when you are in a job interview. In addition, make a video of yourself answering some of the commonly asked questions. This provides the opportunity to gain insight into how you appear to an employer and will help you be ready should you be required to participate in a video interview.

## Research Companies

Take time to research companies you are interested in working for. Look at whether they are currently hiring (some companies will continue to hire during a pandemic). If they are hiring, send your résumé and other required materials for jobs that you are qualified for. If they are not hiring during the pandemic, learn about the company and connect with the hiring manager or other decision makers on LinkedIn. Follow the company's progress so when it is time to interview, you will have up-to-date knowledge about them.

Remember to stay positive. The job search may take longer during a pandemic, and you might have to start out with a part-time or temporary position. However, with a strong résumé and LinkedIn profile, a well-written cover letter and good recommendations, you have the tools to find a job.

# Sources

The five trademarks of agile organizations—McKinsey:

https://www.mckinsey.com/business-functions/
organization/our-insights/the-five-trademarks-of-agile-
organizations

Transitioning to the future of work and the workplace—
Deloitte:

https://www2.deloitte.com/us/en/pages/human-capital/
articles/transitioning-to-the-future-of-work-and-the-
workplace.html